Why the Christian Right Is Wrong

Why the Christian Right Is Wrong

A Minister's Manifesto for Taking Back Your Faith, Your Flag, Your Future

Robin Meyers

JOSSEY-BASS
A Wiley Imprint
www.josseybass.com

Published by Jossey-Bass
A Wiley Imprint
989 Market Street, San Francisco, CA 94103-1741   www.josseybass.com

Jossey-Bass books and products are available through most bookstores. To contact Jossey-Bass directly call our Customer Care Department within the U.S. at 800-956-7739, outside the U.S. at 317-572-3986, or fax 317-572-4002.

Jossey-Bass also publishes its books in a variety of electronic formats. Some content that appears in print may not be available in electronic books.

Library of Congress Cataloging-in-Publication Data

Meyers, Robin R. (Robin Rex), date.
    Why the Christian right is wrong: a minister's manifesto for taking back your faith, your flag, your future / Robin Meyers.
        p. cm.
    Includes bibliographical references.
    ISBN-13: 978-0-7879-8446-5 (cloth)
    ISBN-10: 0-7879-8446-9 (cloth)
        1. Fundamentalism—United States. 2. Conservatism—Religious aspects—Christianity.
3. Conservatism—United States. 4. Christianity and politics—United States. 5. Church and state—United States. 6. United States—Church history—20th century. I. Title.
    BT82.2.M57 2006
    277.3'083—dc22   2006004548

Printed in the United States of America
FIRST EDITION
HB Printing 10 9 8 7 6 5 4 3 2 1

Contents

To my three children,
Blue, Chelsea, and Cass,
and the next generation,
from whom we have borrowed the future

Introduction
The 9/11 Effect

When the twin towers came crashing down on that bright, terrible September morning, most Americans were horrified at first, and then we were angry. It was immediately called "an act of war," even though the old definition hardly applies. At first, we groped in the darkness of trauma for a reason why. The most important question was also the most difficult to ask: *Why do they hate us so much?*

A few brave souls dared to ask it, even fewer brave preachers, because most Americans were in no mood to sound self-incriminating. Introspection, after all, is no match for the purple monster of rage. To ask why is to admit the possibility of cause, and cause suggests complicity. If we are the innocent victim of vast, impersonal forces, then we can assuage our guilt with the illusion that evil can arise in a vacuum and that hatred can spring forth as a fully formed adult without the abuses of childhood.

Hatred, however, is not natural, nor is evil an inherited condition—despite centuries of Christian preaching to the contrary. Hatred is born of parents with names like Envy and Self-Pity. It is hatched in the sibling rivalries of Isaac and Ishmael. It is nurtured by the most powerful force ever to face down love and win: *fear*.

Even so, the first thing that Americans felt after 9/11 wasn't fear or hatred so much as an overwhelming sense that life is utterly unpredictable and that tomorrow is promised to no one. For a few days, with all the planes grounded, the sky itself fell silent. Life was suspended for a moment in the parenthesis of tragedy. Suddenly, the most important thing of all was to be with family and loved ones and to know that they were safe. Emily Dickinson had it right, as usual: "After great pain a formal feeling comes."

There was another feeling, however, that was much more difficult to talk about. As the rhetoric of vengeance grew louder, and a blinding patriotism swept the nation, some of us felt a different emotion, and it was unmistakable. The feeling was *dread*. Almost before the dust had settled, I knew that we were being put to the test. It was a test that required greatness in a president and the capacity for real sacrifice from the rest of us. Therefore, it was a test we were doomed to fail. What's more, at just the moment when we needed the virtues of true faith, we were in grave danger of getting religion at its worst.

This moment of suspended animation was like a crack in time, when all the idols of American life seemed to evaporate and existence itself seemed briefly, poignantly precious. But it did not last long. We quickly resumed the crude pastime of buying and selling one another. The violent movies that we had stopped making for a few months came back, and once again we cheered mindless death and destruction.

What's more, the enormous sympathy of the rest of the world, which held us in prayer through candlelight vigils and soulful solidarity, got left at the altar of history like a jilted bride. For a brief moment, we had experienced a global solidarity as the good will that is born of shared grief made ready partners out of the citizens of the world. The international community stood ready to join us in the greatest manhunt in history. Justice demanded that the perpetrators of this horrific crime be caught and prosecuted because, in an hour so dark, people all over the world said they felt like Americans. They lit their candles and marched. They prayed. They offered their resources in the battle against terrorism. But in the end, we left them standing there—their candles burned out—with no way to help, save the sacrifice of their troops in what would become a disastrous war.

In Washington, a secretive and arrogant administration had closed its doors and started resurrecting a long dormant plan for the preemptive use of military force. A Washington-based think tank called the Project for the New American Century, created in 1997, had already laid the groundwork for a new global American empire. Considered too radical at first for its advocacy of unilateral military force, the neoconservatives who dreamed up this new vision of *Pax Americana* had long waited for what they called "some catastrophic and catalyzing event—like a new Pearl Harbor."[1]

Only thirteen days after 9/11, the USA PATRIOT Act was formally submitted to Congress and passed on October 26 while both Congress and the American people were still in shock, and then we were called upon to circle the wagons, get back to shopping, and prepare to let the world know that nobody, but nobody "messes with the *USA* and gets away with it!"

At no time are human beings more malleable than when they are afraid. The test of a great leader is to *discourage* appeals to fear and to exhort the nation to hope, to courage, and to the rejection of vengeance. When FDR said, "The only thing we have to fear is fear itself," he could just as well have been inscribing the epitaph on a postmodern American tombstone. Now, it seems, *the only thing we have to fear more than terrorism is fear of terrorism itself*.

When I rose to preach in my own pulpit on the Sunday after 9/11, it felt sadly reminiscent of a day not long before when a clean-cut young Marine named Timothy McVeigh used a homemade truck bomb to bring down the Alfred P. Murrah Federal Building, killing 168 of my friends and neighbors. In Oklahoma City, we know something about the fruits of hatred.

Unfortunately, we also share a distinctly American disease, and it can be fatal. We confuse justice and vengeance. A civilized response to tragedy, after all, should be recognizably different, especially for those who claim to know that "those who live by the sword shall die by the sword." What I prayed for that first Sunday after 9/11 was "an unearthly patience" and the wisdom of God, not the wisdom of Machiavelli—"lest countless more innocent people die."

Looking back on it, the dread I felt that morning was sadly prophetic. Countless more innocents have now been killed than died on 9/11. The nation I love has rolled back civil liberties, divided the world up into good guys and "evildoers," and squandered the goodwill of our allies. The president's response to the legitimate hesitation of the United Nations was to say, in effect, either you're with us or you're "irrelevant."[2]

More frightening still, the dread I felt was not confined to politics. It was a dread about the future of religion in America as well. The twin forces of hatred and fear have now stoked the bonfires of religious bigotry and given Christian fundamentalists what they most desire: a common enemy and the newest face of evil. In the world according to such Christian Right luminaries as James Dobson, Jerry Falwell, and Pat Robertson, the "enemy" is all nonbelievers, and the devil is that amoral monster called "secular humanism."

It lurks just outside the door of America's mythical little house on the prairie. Inside are the chosen; outside are feminist barbarians, abortionists, gays, gun control advocates, environmentalists, agnostics, college professors, tattooed free thinkers, sexual hedonists, UN sympathizers, and, of course, Democrats—the party that dances with the devil because it still cares about poor people.

Once that door is broken down, we are told, the unarmed innocents inside will be destroyed. The women will be raped, their Bibles will be burned, and the children will be turned into homosexuals. Because secular humanists do not have "moral clarity," we are now on a slippery slope that ends in moral chaos. Legions of Bible-quoting fundamentalists must lead the charge in what they believe to be a cosmic battle for the future of Western civilization. There will be no treaties. No compromise. It's winner take all.

What the rational world must now understand is that the forces against which we struggle are not rational. In fact, they view logic itself as seductive and dangerous. Fundamentalists, by definition, are not content to "live and let live." *Everyone must be converted.* If "nonbelievers" fail to see the light, they will spend eternity regretting it. Therefore, the lives of the nonconverted are clearly expendable.

September 11, 2001, gave Christian fundamentalists (who would prefer that we not use that word anymore) the perfect vision of a dark and chaotic future. They could claim that the sky was literally falling and that God really does punish evildoers. What's more, politicians and their corporate owners could co-opt this fear, join forces with Christian conservatives, and form what is commonly called the Christian Right—a potent new voting bloc for the Republican party.

Throughout this book, I will be using the term *Christian Right* to define a powerful but complicated political movement in America. Although the term is often used to describe all conservative Christians and their political leanings, there are many evangelical Christians who do not share the agenda of the Christian Right, and some nonevangelicals who do. The Christian Right has been dominated by Protestants but also includes conservative Catholics, Jews, Mormons, and occasionally secularists.

Many evangelicals and fundamentalists decided in the 1980s and '90s to abandon their long-standing tendency to shun "faith-based" political action. Urged on by a new generation of TV preachers who declared that all things liberal were now all things evil, the faithful got up out of their pews and voted en masse for what they believed were "God's candidates." Estimates of the number of such voters who can be galvanized by specific issues like abortion and gun control ranges from 35 to 60 million.

Although they are far from identical in background or doctrine, they share a remarkably similar view that the Bible constitutes the immutable moral foundation of Western society and consider traditional Christian beliefs to be under siege from a host of "enemies." Higher criticism in seminaries constitutes a threat to biblical inerrancy, as does the teaching of evolution in schools.

But the seeds of the Christian Right were actually sown in the tumultuous decade of the 1960s, when civil rights, women's liberation, the sexual revolution, and the reemergence of Eastern religious ideas seemed to shift the moral universe on its axis. Supreme Court decisions banning compulsory prayer in schools, legalizing abortion, and protecting the wall between church and state stirred a deep resentment in many conservative Christians and their non-Christian sympathizers.

When charismatic figures like Jerry Falwell, Pat Robertson, and Phyllis Schlafly began organizing a mass media defense of what they considered "traditional Christian values," the Christian Right soon became a potent political machine. There is a broad consensus that the Christian Right was the deciding factor in the election and re-election of George W. Bush. After all, leaders of the Christian Right told their legions that it was a holy mandate: "I believe it is the responsibility of every political conservative," said Jerry Falwell, "every evangelical Christian, every pro-life Catholic, every traditional Jew, every Reagan Democrat, and everyone in between to get serious about re-electing President Bush."[3]

Even so, it must be clearly understood that there is both a Christian Right and a political Right, and the two are not identical. When I refer to the Christian Right, I will be referring to this broad, energized, theocratic voting bloc that has taken the media and much of the American public by surprise. Having provided a crucial "base" for the political Right, the two have now formed an uneasy and unholy alliance. Not all Republicans are fundamentalists, but virtually all fundamentalists are Republicans. As Bill Moyers astutely noted, the GOP is now, for all practical purposes, a theocracy—"God's Own Party," as the faithful put it.[4]

The worldview of the Christian Right is based on moral absolutes (spelled out primarily in what is believed to be an infallible Bible) regarding the fixity of sexual identity, the moral superiority of capitalism, and the sanctity of unborn life. Adherents believe that the government should cultivate virtue but not interfere in the marketplace or the workplace. What's more, the lazy and the lawless should never be compensated by the proceeds or sympathies of the hardworking or the law-abiding.

The Christian Right has identified what it believes to be the greatest threat to morality: the illusion that ethical issues can be *contextual* and evolving. It has organized itself to do fervent battle against all moral "relativists" and does so by quoting selected Scripture removed from its historical context. A common characteristic of the Religious Right is the fear that any hole in the moral dyke will ultimately lead to the collapse of the entire moral structure and thus Western civilization itself. It is therefore safer to embrace an unambiguous "moral clarity" than to think too much, ask too many questions, or employ the tenets of cogent reasoning.

Now that the Republican Party and the Christian Right have become one seamless political machine, they are taking no prisoners. With a Bible in one hand and a voter guide in the other, the political Right is firmly in control of two branches of government and has its sights set on the third, the judiciary, the last bastion of reason and respect for the separation of church and state. Even though the life appointment process was intended to make the courts the most apolitical entity left in the Republic, judges often make rulings that frustrate the Christian Right because they are not based on "biblical law." For this reason, judges are considered the "new enemy."[5] They are all that stand in the way of an American theocracy.

Two years ago, in newspaper columns, on the radio, and from the pulpit, I began applying the term *Christian fascism* to the direction in which America is headed. Some of my friends and colleagues found the terminology too strong. Others called it "deeply offensive." But when Oklahoma Senator Tom Cole's chief of staff recently said that we should not just impeach judges who make the wrong decisions, but "impale them,"[6] more people have started using the *f*-word without apology.

Fascism, after all, comes in many guises. It was once brown shirts, banned books, and the Holocaust. But it can take many forms, so long as vested interests control the government. All that is required is a nation full of uninformed people whose religion makes them more fearful than enlightened. Fascism thrives on a worldview that is black and white and co-opts the name of a partisan God to fight crusades that pretend to be about moral values but are in fact about preserving and protecting wealth and power.

Christian fascism corrupts both politics and religion by stifling political dissent and debate and by regarding kindness and compassion, the heart of religious faith, as naive. It dresses up as the savior of Western civilization, asking the rest of us to place our trust in the ability of the Appointed Ones to defend us while actually turning back the clock of human progress.

What's more, the heart and soul of Christianity itself gets hijacked in the process. Choosing to wage war instead of avoiding it if at all possible is *unthinkable* for a follower of the Prince of Peace. Demonizing the "other" in order to enrich oneself and protect a patronage system with revolving doors and no-bid contracts is exactly the kind of pious hypocrisy that the Rabbi from Nazareth railed against. Now has the peculiar and radical claim of the Gospel that "God is made perfect in weakness" become unrecognizable in an age of Warrior Jesus and Locker Room Christianity.

So let there be no mistake. This is the world to which my children, and the next generation, has now awakened. It's a world in which nothing is what it seems to be and reality itself is choreographed by corporate media with their eye on the bottom line. It's a world in which the soldiers we idolize slaughter a faceless brown enemy in the ancient cradle of civilization, and the Tigris and Euphrates Rivers now carry floating corpses past piles of rubble.

Meanwhile, back home, you wouldn't know there was a war going on. We are too busy discussing celebrity trials and antiaging creams. Should Jesus of Nazareth return and make a triumphal entry into Washington, D.C., he would surely weep again, saying, "You [still] do not know the things which make for peace."

The dreaded military-industrial complex that the departing President Eisenhower warned us about has now lost the hyphen and become one word. We cut taxes on the rich and pass the cost of a misbegotten war on to our children. We fiddle with fashion, trumpet gossip, and hawk get-rich-quick schemes while our own empire, our *Pax Americana*, burns. We are sleepwalking through a desert of lost conscience.

All of this can be chalked up to the ranting of a liberal minister, of course. When in doubt, just claim that your opponent is part of the enemy camp. But this all goes much deeper than partisan politics. In the church where this reputedly "Christian" nation still worships, we claim to be the disciples of a man who got so angry once that he overturned the furniture in the Temple and drove the moneychangers out with a whip. So much for Sweet Jesus, "meek and mild . . . gentle as a little child."

Besides, I have spent my whole life trying to persuade people that *liberal* is not a dirty word and that Christianity is a way of life, not a set of creeds and doctrines demanding total agreement. I've also pointed out that our electoral process is broken and corrupt and our politicians have become part televangelist, part lobbyist, and part independent contractor. What I did not know until recently, however, was that so many other Americans feel *exactly the same way*. They just needed someone to put their frustration into words.

That opportunity finally came my way, disguised as an "ordinary" event—a brief speech that I was invited to deliver at a peace rally on the campus of the University of Oklahoma. It was, in fact, the beginning of a life-changing event, and this book is the continuation of that speech. It is an elaboration of the grievances that struck such a deep chord in the hearts and minds of so many Americans. It is the fulfillment of my promise to rally like-minded citizens to take action to save the church that so many of us love but feel deserted by and the country we all call home but hardly recognize anymore.

It's the story of the power of the Internet and the resilient goodwill of countless forgotten Americans who are saddened by the arrogance and violence of our time. My intent is to fan the flames of a fire that is already burning and to remind those who would lead us that "we the people" still hold the power, and the consent of the governed will no longer be taken for granted when the government itself is corrupt.

Simply put, my speech was only the beginning of something much, much bigger than one man's opinion or one minister's attempt to speak truth to power. It is the beginning of what must become a proactive, systematic, courageous movement in America— a call to nonviolent resistance, to cultural noncompliance, and to social transformation.

For three simple reasons, the revolution starts here. The emperor is naked. The flag is flying upside down. And Jesus has been silenced by his own church.

Why the Christian Right Is Wrong

Part One

The Speech Heard
Round the World

The invitation came after the November 2004 election, when half the country felt clinically depressed about the reelection of George W. Bush. People in the blue states were feeling blue, but "folks" in the red states, like my native Oklahoma, were thumping their suspenders. A giant billboard on the expressway in my hometown of Oklahoma City said it best: W: STILL THE PRESIDENT! OUR PRAYERS ARE WITH YOU!

Meanwhile, a group of students at the University of Oklahoma were planning a peace rally and candlelight vigil to protest the war in Iraq. They were looking for a speaker who could express the growing frustration they felt, and a rising tide of Americans now feel, about the lies that led us into this misbegotten war—and the tide of human blood it has unleashed.

What was different about this rally, however, was the sponsor. United Campus Ministry, an ecumenical religious organization that promotes interfaith understanding and protects second opinions in the Bible Belt, organized the event. This is no easy task in Oklahoma, where Christian triumphalism reigns, football is the golden calf, Jesus is a warrior, and Democrats are considered "peculiar."

A member of my congregation, Sean Emerson, brought the invitation on behalf of Laura Culbertson. Mayflower Congregational Church, the United Church of Christ (UCC) congregation I have led for twenty years, is known as an outpost of liberal Protestantism in Oklahoma. Its Web site (http://mayflowerucc.org) bears the banner "Unapologetically Christian, Unapologetically Liberal." We are an "Open and Affirming" congregation[1] and regard the essence of the Gospel to be an "extravagant welcome" that compels us to make room at the table for everyone and wage peace by working for justice.

Granted, this is not the majority approach in Oklahoma, and so the list of potential liberal speakers is a short one. I have been asked to speak at many such gatherings and am always grateful if the crowd is larger than the organizing committee! But in this case, something else was going on. Something had begun to dawn on many of us that goes beyond politics and is much deeper and more insidious than sour grapes after the election.

This wasn't just a group of old hippies, trying to warn the next generation about another Vietnam. It was a room full of young people whose silence has left the impression that to be a person of faith is automatically to be considered a wholly owned subsidiary of the Christian Right. The organizers of the rally wanted an ordained minister to speak to something just as frightening as the web of deceptions that led us to war: the hijacking of the Christian faith.

After the trauma of 9/11, and using fear as a weapon to silence critics and question their patriotism, the Bush administration has managed to choreograph more than just the illusion of a successful presidency. It has given the Christian Right a seat at the table of government power that is unprecedented.[2] To cultivate and energize its political base, the administration has embraced tactics that many of us consider antithetical to religion—hatred, paranoia, arrogance, greed, and the fine art of demonizing the other—all in the name of a penniless rabbi from Nazareth who preached love, faith, humility, generosity, and the nonjudgmental acceptance of the other.

Now nothing is what it seems to be. If the word *Orwellian* had not been so overused, it would finally have the impact that it deserves. We live in a bubble of macho rhetoric that is a joke around the world, and we continue to act as if there is something endearing about ignorance. A Baptist minister in North Carolina puts up a sign in his church that says that the Koran ought to be flushed down the toilet—and takes it down and apologizes only after a storm of bad publicity.[3]

Moral Majority founder Jerry Falwell claims that 9/11 was a punishment by God for all our heathen activity, especially our tolerance of homosexuality, while remaining silent on the devastation caused by hurricane after hurricane striking the state of Florida. James Dobson, of the powerful Christian Right lobby Focus on the Family, calls the justices of the Supreme Court "terrorists in black robes" after the Terri Schiavo decision proclaiming that the government did not have the right to overrule next of kin when it comes to making end-of-life health care decisions, forgetting that he had once praised them for their role in selecting Bush to be president after the 2000 election because it was "God's will."

Intent on "saving marriage" by denying it to gays in committed relationships, multiply divorced and extramaritally "active" preachers have forgotten how nontraditional the "family values" of Jesus were. So far as we know, he never married and never counseled his followers to marry. But most of all, the Christian Right seems to have forgotten that Jesus saved his white-hot anger for the sin of religious hypocrisy.

Clicking through the TV wasteland of so-called religious programming is like watching a *Saturday Night Live* skit as hucksters with big hair peddle prosperity theology as the payoff for faith. All over the country, megachurch pastors exhort their followers to invest in Jesus by giving "a love gift to support this ministry"—and then to expect "financial freedom" as proof that God loves them.

Faith healer Benny Hinn brings his "crusade" to my city and choreographs the illusion of healing in a fraudulent spectacle that preys on the sick, the desperate, and the lonely. Before he arrives in his white suit and diamond rings, our ultraconservative, family-values-touting newspaper, *The Oklahoman*, takes his money and runs a full-page ad to swell the ranks of the gullible.

Meanwhile, so-called lovers of Jesus trash the environment, scoff at global warming, swear their undying allegiance to Israel (no matter how its government behaves), and await the Second Coming as the ultimate way to handle guilt. Why be concerned about a *Silent Spring,* after all, when all the really important people have already gone home to be with Jesus the Jew?

Just think of it. The Christian Right now has its arms wrapped tightly around Israel—for military and economic reasons, of course, but also because it is believed to be, by some tortured interpretation of Revelation, the staging ground for an apocalypse that ultimately leaves the Jews behind! In the wildly popular series of "Left Behind" books, the Prince of Peace, the Good Shepherd, the Light of the World returns to melt the flesh off the bones of unbelievers.[4]

How did we get here? Does anybody care? Shouldn't we at least jump up and down and scream before the country we love goes fascist?

To my way of thinking, the most poignant bumper sticker in the land is the one that says, "If you aren't completely appalled, then you haven't been paying attention!" More frightening than the corruption of both our cherished democratic ideals and the co-opting of Jesus to get votes is the fact that so many of us don't seem to care. Are we too busy watching celebrity trials or gawking at Hollywood couples to read, to think, to fight back against an avalanche of propaganda?

With this in mind, and more, I sat down in a coffee shop in Norman, Oklahoma, to jot down a few notes for my speech. I was so troubled by what was happening that the words seemed to flow onto the page effortlessly. It was a litany of lament. It was a wake-up call.

I knew that it needed to be provocative but not incendiary. It needed to challenge the most basic assumptions of what constitutes morality in our time without being obscene or full of juvenile ad hominem attacks. Perhaps, in fact, it only needed to be true, because truth is the strangest thing of all these days.

Although I had said many of these things before, in newspaper columns, from the pulpit, and in radio commentaries for National Public Radio, I had no idea that the speech I was about to give would become an Internet phenomenon and the subject of a national and even international debate.

At first I thought I was just "preaching to the choir," as we say in the church. Little did I know how big the audience would turn out to be. Crowded into that room on that rainy night in Norman were about 150 students, some with their parents, some with their professors, and some who were just curious to hear what a liberal minister in Oklahoma might say and debate whether this is an oxymoron.

A band made up of Jewish, Christian, and Muslim musicians warmed up the crowd. Interfaith prayers for peace were offered, and then I was introduced. I took my notes to the microphone and spoke the following words.

As some of you know, I am minister of Mayflower Congregational UCC Church in Oklahoma City, an open and affirming, peace and justice church in northwest Oklahoma City, and professor of rhetoric at Oklahoma City University. But you would most likely have encountered me on the pages of the *Oklahoma Gazette,* where I have been a columnist for six years and hold the record for most number of angry letters to the editor.

Tonight I join the ranks of those who are angry, because I have watched as the faith I love has been taken over by fundamentalists who claim to speak for Jesus but whose actions are anything but Christian. We're heard a lot lately about so-called moral values as having swung the election to President Bush. Well, I'm a great believer in moral values, but we need to have a discussion, all over this country, about exactly what constitutes a moral value—I mean, what are we talking about? Because we don't get to make them up as we go along, especially not if we are people of faith. We have an *inherited* tradition of what is right and wrong, and moral is as moral does. Let me give you just a few of the reasons why I take issue with those in power who claim that moral values are on their side.

When you start a war on false pretenses and then act as if your deceptions are justified because you are doing God's will and that your critics are either unpatriotic or lacking in faith, there are some of us who have given our lives to teaching and preaching the faith who believe that this is not only not moral but immoral.

When you live in a country that has established international rules for waging a just war, built the United Nations on your own soil to enforce them, and then arrogantly break the very rules you set down for the rest of the world, you are doing something immoral.

When you claim that Jesus is the Lord of your life and yet fail to acknowledge that your policies ignore his essential teaching or turn them on their head (you know, Sermon on the Mount stuff like never returning violence for violence and those who live by the sword will die by the sword), you are doing something immoral.

When you act as if the lives of Iraqi civilians are not as important as the lives of American soldiers and refuse to even count them, you are doing something immoral.

When you find a way to avoid combat in Vietnam and then question the patriotism of someone who volunteered to fight and came home a hero, you are doing something immoral.

When you ignore the fundamental teachings of the Gospels, which say that the way the strong treat the weak is the ultimate ethical test, by giving tax breaks to the wealthiest among us so that the strong will get stronger and the weak will get weaker, you are doing something immoral.

When you wink at the torture of prisoners and deprive so-called enemy combatants of the rules of the Geneva Convention, which your own country helped establish and insists that other countries follow, you are doing something immoral.

When you claim that the world can be divided up into the good guys and the "evildoers," slice up your own nation into those who are with you or with the terrorists—and then launch a war that enriches your own friends and seizes control of the oil to which we are addicted instead of helping us kick the habit, you are doing something immoral.

When you fail to veto a single spending bill but ask us to pay for a war with no exit strategy and no end in sight, creating an enormous deficit that hangs like a great millstone around the necks of our children, you are doing something immoral.

When you cause most of the rest of the world to hate a country that was once the most loved country in the world and act as if it doesn't matter what others think of us, only what God thinks of you, you have done something immoral.

When you use hatred of homosexuals as a wedge issue to turn out record numbers of evangelical voters and seek to use the Constitution as a tool of discrimination, you are doing something immoral.

When you favor the death penalty and yet claim to be a follower of Jesus, who said an eye for an eye was the old way, not the way of the Kingdom, you are doing something immoral.

When you dismantle countless environmental laws designed to protect the earth, which is God's gift to us all, so that the corporations that bought you and paid for your favors will make higher profits while our children breathe dirty air and live in a toxic world, you have done something immoral. The earth belongs to the Lord, not Halliburton.

When you claim that our God is bigger than their God and that our killing is righteous while theirs is evil, we have begun to resemble the enemy we claim to be fighting, and that is immoral. We have met the enemy, and the enemy is us.

When you tell people that you intend to run and govern as a "compassionate conservative," using a word that is the essence of all religious faith—*compassion*—and then show no compassion for anyone who disagrees with you and no patience with those who cry to you for help, you are doing something immoral.

When you talk constantly about Jesus, who was a healer of the sick, but do nothing to make sure that anyone who is sick can go to see a doctor, even if she doesn't have a penny in her pocket, you are doing something immoral.

When you put judges on the bench who are racist and will set women back a hundred years, and when you surround yourself with preachers who say gays ought to be killed, you are doing something immoral.

I'm tired of people thinking that because I'm a Christian, I must be a supporter of President Bush, or that because I favor civil rights and gay rights, I must not be a person of faith. I'm tired of people saying that I can't support the troops but oppose the war.

I heard that when I was your age, when the Vietnam war was raging. We knew that that war was wrong, and you know that this war is wrong—the only question is how many people are going to die before these make-believe Christians are removed from power.

This country is bankrupt. The war is morally bankrupt. The claim of this administration to be Christian is bankrupt. And the only people who can turn things around are people like you—young people who are just beginning to wake up to what is happening to them. It's your country to take back. It's your faith to take back. It's your future to take back.

Don't be afraid to speak out. Don't back down when your friends begin to tell you that the cause is righteous and that the flag should be wrapped around the cross while the rest of us keep our mouths shut. Real Christians take chances for peace. So do real Jews and real Muslims and real Hindus and real Buddhists; so do all the faith traditions of the world at their heart believe one thing: life is precious.

Every human being is precious. Arrogance is the opposite of faith. Greed is the opposite of charity. And believing that one has never made a mistake is the mark of a deluded man, not a man of faith.

As for war, war is the greatest failure of the human race—and thus the greatest failure of faith. There's an old rock song whose lyrics say it all: "War, what is it good for? Absolutely nothing."

And what is the dream of the prophets? That we should study war no more, that we should beat our swords into plowshares and our spears into pruning hooks. Who would Jesus bomb indeed? How many wars does it take to know that too many people have died? What if they gave a war and nobody came? Maybe one day we will find out.

Time to march again, my friends. Time to commit acts of nonviolent civil disobedience. My generation finally stopped a tragic war. Yours can too.

After the speech ended and the participants walked quietly around the campus in a candlelight vigil, several students asked me if they could have a copy of my remarks. I gave them my notes, and they must have gone back to their dorm rooms and transcribed them. A member of the band said he was going to send the speech to a friend in Germany. Others must have sent it to their friends and family—or perhaps to their parents to help them understand what they were feeling. Others sent it to their professors so that they would hear a second opinion. We live in a divided land, and often this subject cannot be discussed at the dinner table. One sentiment recurred countless times in the subject line and in the opening lines of countless e-mails: "This is exactly what I've been feeling, and now someone has put it into words."

In a matter of weeks, with people sending it to everyone in their address book, who then sent it to everyone in their address book, the speech was suddenly everywhere online. I have received hundreds and hundreds of letters and e-mails—from all fifty states and numerous foreign countries. The speech has appeared on countless blogs and been debated, line by line, from both the Left and the Right. I've heard from Americans of all ages, from all walks of life, and from every conceivable religious persuasion. A young Republican lawyer in California wrote to say that he had advised the administration at the university where I teach that they should consider my employment a liability. Should any harm come to any students as a result of my call to civil disobedience, he wrote, the university should consider itself liable.

The speech carried no title, so readers came up with their own, to suit their own understanding of what it meant to them. The most common title by far: "What Are Moral Values?"

Many people wrote to ask me if the document was real or a fake, given that it was reputed to be a speech given by a minister from Oklahoma. Hundreds of newspapers asked for permission to reprint the speech, and I gave them all carte blanche, at no charge. I wanted to get the message out and to see how far the Internet chain would stretch.

When the e-mails first started coming, a trickle soon turned into an avalanche. The university set up an automated response site to handle the volume and keep the university server from crashing. I tried to answer all the e-mails personally, because the vast majority of letters were overwhelmingly positive, and many were deeply moving. I gave up when that task began to consume more hours every day than I could give, and I apologize to all those who never got an adequate response.

This book is my response to all of you, and I offer it with gratitude, and with a sense of urgency, to the millions of my fellow Americans who are just now waking up to a new and disturbing reality. The country we love, and the church that has inspired and nurtured so many of us, is in grave peril.

Part Two

The Sin of Hypocrisy:
Line by Line

Chapter One

Christians Don't Start Wars, They Try to Stop Them

When you start a war on false pretenses and then act as if your deceptions are justified because you are doing God's will and that your critics are either unpatriotic or lacking in faith, there are some of us who have given our lives to teaching and preaching the faith who believe that this is not only not moral, but immoral.

If the whole, terrible, wretched truth could be known about the Iraq war—in one blinding, bloody moment like looking into the sun without blinking—anyone with a conscience would turn away and vomit. In the moments that follow, in the empty, clarifying calm that comes just after, such a person would begin to feel something else. The sadness would be joined with righteous indignation, because it is impossible to love the world and not hate what destroys it.

For every fallen soldier, for every dark-eyed Iraqi girl and boy, for every wailing mother wandering in the carnage of the latest bombing, the only truly religious response to an unnecessary war is rage. Until we feel it, and do not for a moment confuse our fears with our faith, there can be nothing that approaches righteousness in us.

Even though we are not allowed to see the flag-draped coffins coming home or the true horror that is this tragic misadventure, we can see it in the "imagination of our hearts." And because we can, there should be "neither rest nor tranquillity," as Dr. King would say, "until justice rolls down like water, and righteousness like a mighty stream."[1]

It is one thing to be dragged reluctantly into the horror that is war to stop a tyrant like Adolf Hitler. It is entirely another to have already decided on "regime change" in Iraq for personal, political, or economic reasons and then to engineer civilian consent through an elaborate hoax.

Former Treasury Secretary Paul O'Neill removed any doubt about when the Iraq war was planned when he turned over nineteen thousand internal memos to former *Wall Street Journal* reporter Ron Suskind. Suskind's book *The Price of Loyalty* revealed that at the very first National Security Council meeting, held just ten days after the inauguration and eight months before 9/11, the topic of conversation in the Bush administration was how to get rid of Saddam Hussein. O'Neill put it bluntly. "It was all about finding a way to do it. That was the tone of it. The President saying, 'Go find me a way to do this.'"[2]

One memo was marked "Plan for Post-Saddam Iraq," and another was titled "Foreign Suitors for Iraqi Oilfield Contracts." After campaigning against "nation building" and overextending our troops during the Clinton administration, Bush did exactly the opposite. The most overtly "religious" president in U.S. history, running to "restore integrity to the White House," had already decided on a preemptive invasion of Iraq and then went in search of a reason to give the American people for sending their sons and daughters to die. It wasn't about the oil, of course.

The first premise for the war was to protect us against the "imminent threat" represented by Iraq's possession of weapons of mass destruction. There were none. Next we were told that Iraq and al-Qaeda were "operationally linked," but that wasn't true either, as the administration has now admitted. So this war in search of a reason moved into yet more abstract territory. We were "defending our freedom," even though it was never threatened. And we were "spreading freedom and democracy throughout the region," even though life in Iraq is now more desperate, more deadly, and less hopeful than ever.

History will record this war, and the lies that led us into it, as one of the great foreign policy blunders in American history. The most amazing fact of all is that the president still has his job. To add insult to death, the Bush administration has co-opted the sympathies of the Christian Right by representing itself as a crusader for Christian moral principles. Yet this war does not begin to satisfy the requirement of the church's just-war theory. What's more, individuals who prey on our fears or bear false witness can never call themselves faithful.

Anyone who still doubts that a new American military imperialism was on the drawing board long before 9/11 and waiting for what neoconservatives called "a Pearl Harbor moment" has not read a word put out by the Project for the New American Century (PNAC). The brainchild of William Kristol and Robert Kagan, PNAC aimed to put the United States back on a course toward "global leadership" where America accepts its "unique role in preserving and extending an international order friendly to our security, our prosperity, and our principles."[3] From its inception in 1997, the Holy Grail of the group was to remove Saddam Hussein from power.

Someone once said that "the opposite of love is not hate; it's fear." If that's true, then Bush policy adviser Condoleezza Rice employed it masterfully when she raised the most frightening specter to the modern mind. Before the war, she said, "The problem here is that there will always be some uncertainty about how quickly [Saddam] can acquire nuclear weapons. But we don't want the smoking gun to be a mushroom cloud."[4]

Never mind that we have yet to find a smoking gun, polls consistently showed that the choreographed lie linking Iraq to 9/11 worked, as polls indicated that two-thirds of the American people bought it at first. Now we are left to wonder what the real reasons were, and that is a much more complicated matter. Was the son trying to finish his father's business, or was a wealthy oilman surrounded by other wealthy oilmen simply seizing control of the world's second-largest supply of sweet crude? This much is certain: a trusting and patriotic nation was hoodwinked.

To press the point that our "enemy" was beyond redemption (which is a strangely un-Christian idea), Bush's clumsy public disclaimers about not meaning to disparage a whole race or religion could not compete with the broad brush of his "evildoer" rhetoric. Again and again we were told that 9/11 was the result of the fact that "they hate our freedom," rather than allowing for the possibility that the attacks grew out of a pathological hatred toward the West for centuries of anti-Arab policy and a militant effort to globalize Western cultural and religious values. For the average American listening to the president speak, the message was as clear as it was fallacious: *an Arab is an Arab is a terrorist, and this is a holy war.*

But never fear. We have a free press, do we not—protected by the Constitution—to save us from just such an abuse of power? Think again. If anyone still doubts that we live in perilous times, just consider that after the nation finally learned the identity of Deep Throat, whose secret testimony in the Watergate scandal brought down another president who abused the executive branch, a judge ordered two reporters to reveal their confidential sources, and Judith Miller of the *New York Times* went to jail rather than comply. *Time* magazine management then caved in, claiming that "no one is above the law." Had those reporters been named Woodward and Bernstein, or had the *Washington Post* caved in, Nixon would never have resigned in disgrace, and the nation would never have known the truth.

Now the question is a deeper and more disturbing one: do people even want to *know* the truth? Desiring the truth would require that we be honest about ourselves and our complicity in the evils we deplore. It would mean taking stock of the ways in which we have turned greed from a deadly sin to an American virtue and coddled rampant individualism with a therapeutic vengeance.

It would require that we refuse to allow media outlets to be entertainment subsidiaries of major corporations so that we get independent journalism again and not right-wing "infotainment" or electronic voyeurism. Had Fox News been around in 1974, the Watergate scandal would have been the subject of a round-the-clock smear campaign, with Bill O'Reilly and Sean Hannity calling it an "outrageous attack on the presidency, our nation, and the values we hold dear." Viewers would then have been invited to call in and register their anger, answering the question, "Should this investigation go forward or not? You decide."

Rush Limbaugh tells his "ditto-heads" that Democrats (and implicitly everyone on the Left) "are more fearful of Christians than they are of al-Qaeda."[5] But it would be more accurate to say that most of us fear war more than we fear sex, which appears to be the only grounds for impeachment these days. To the Right, lying about sex (a sin of weakness and shame) is apparently far worse than lying the whole nation into an illegal war (a sin of malice and hubris). Sad as the Clinton scandal was (and exceedingly stupid), it looks particularly tame now by comparison to the bloodletting and terrorist quagmire that the occupation and civil war in Iraq has become.

The Christian Right, which gave George W. Bush his margin of victory and celebrated it as a sign that God had triumphed over White House wickedness, seems to have accepted war as inevitable if regrettable and sex as regrettable if inevitable. These were not the priorities of Jesus, of course, but when was the last time anybody asked, "What would Jesus do?" and regarded it as anything other than a rhetorical exercise?

Jesus didn't talk much about sex. He forgave a woman caught in adultery and reminded her would-be executioners that they were hypocrites. He did not shame her. He also reminded the self-righteous that you can commit adultery in your heart, which Jimmy Carter, perhaps the most authentically Christian president ever, actually confessed to—only to be mercilessly mocked by conservatives.

If you hope to find scriptural support for our culture's obsession with what everyone else is doing in bed, you will be very disappointed. What Jesus did talk about was the failure of public piety to manifest itself in meaningful private compassion. What he warned us about repeatedly was the power of money to seduce and to enslave. It was both a hazard and an obligation. But what made him explode with anger was the sin of talking about God all the time and being publicly ob-servant while maintaining systems that oppressed God's people and robbed them of their dignity. For Jesus, there was no hypocrisy like *religious* hypocrisy.

He healed the sick, with or without insurance, and welcomed the outcast—turning the first-century world of power and privilege upside down. The ease with which he moved among sinners and for-gave them caused his critics to accuse him of moral relativism and cheap grace—the same fears that grip many in the Christian Right today. Without strict rules and swift judgment, they tell us, the world as we know it will come to an end. Spare God's rod of judgment, and the whole of Creation will be spoiled. Where Jesus says "fear not," the message of the Christian Right is just the opposite: "Be afraid. Be very afraid."

It was no mere slip of the tongue that caused the president, only a few days after 9/11, to refer to his war on terrorism as a "crusade" before his handlers moved quickly to apologize.[6] The truth is, that was a rare moment of uncensored honesty. He does indeed believe that his mission is holy and that this war is approved by God. He be-lieves that God has called him, though clumsy of tongue like Moses, to find and fight for the chosen ones against a world of infidels.

But so has every crusader, in every age, believed that his cause was holy. When Bush says, repeatedly, that we must "fight them *there* before we have to fight them *here*," he is confusing Christ with Machiavelli. Preemptive killing, after all, is about as far from loving thy neighbor as one can get.

The sad truth is that in the name of protecting us from terrorists, we have now accelerated the pace at which the world is training ter-rorists. Thanks to the increase in terrorism around the world since the war began, we have lost personal freedoms at home, not "pro-tected them," as the president says ad nauseam. According to a CIA report, Iraq is now the destination of choice for terrorists, where they receive on-the-job training to export their "skills" around the world.[7] Reacting to the deaths of their innocents by pledging to kill ours, the temperature in the terrorist ovens of the world just keeps rising.

One might expect something more out of a "born-again" president than "we'll get you before you get us." "Bring 'em back dead or alive" strikes a deep chord in the American psyche, but it hardly sounds like a man who claims that Jesus is the most important influence on his life. Indeed, the president's taunting West Texas rhetoric, like "Bring 'em on!" makes a strange sound when compared to "Father forgive them, for they know not what they do."

In the end, nothing could be more *irreligious* than to use fear and loathing of the "enemy" and a commitment to vigilante violence as a way of protecting ourselves. We know that in every religious system in the world, true faith is about *breaking* the cycle of violence. When Jesus was arrested in the garden of Gethsemane, the apostles, some of whom were still zealots, drew their swords and offered to fight back. Jesus would have none of it and ordered the weapons put away.

Admitting mistakes and apologizing have always been regarded as signs of weakness in the Bush family, much less "turning the other cheek." The elder President Bush is famous for having said, "I will never apologize for the United States of America. I don't care what the facts are!"[8] What works is fear. Tell the people that you are protecting them, and they will give up their firstborn child. Tell them that you are at war against a new enemy and that you alone have the means and the resolve to defeat that enemy, and they will surrender their freedom, their common sense, and their most basic assumptions about morality.

To silence your critics and sidestep the charge that your method of fighting terrorism not only doesn't work but contradicts the life and message of the Lord, the Bush administration has cloaked the entire misbegotten enterprise in the language of divine destiny. Following in the footsteps of Rome (whose Caesars were considered Sons of God), you must insist that the peace you bring, the *Pax Americana*, is the blessed by-product of an iron fist and that it is better to be feared than to be loved.

Using the rhetoric of "us against them," you can even utter aloud the most dangerous false dichotomy ever to fall from the lips of any occupant of the White House: "Every nation in every region now has a decision to make. Either you're with us, or you are with the terrorists."[9] Such simplistic moral thinking, and Bush's constant use of the word *evil* to demonize the "other," could not be more diametrically opposed to the ministry and message of Jesus.

Wearing religion on his sleeve and patriotism on his lapel, this son of wealth and privilege has mistaken power for righteousness. The Jesus who is reputed to have helped him stop drinking and carousing is much more than a divine personal trainer. He is the radical teacher of an alternative and subversive wisdom. That wisdom, at odds with the power structure of his time and ours, would place Bush in the role of the rich and the merciless in most of the New Testament parables.

Besides, Christianity is not just about reforming bad habits. It is a call to become the beloved community of "resident aliens." Christian morality is not simply a religious strategy for reforming and enriching the individual but rather a call to self-sacrifice in dismantling unjust *systems* in the world that oppress the neighbor. It's not "all about me"; it's "all about the other."

New Testament scholar Marcus Borg has reminded us that Jesus was a spirit-person and a social revolutionary.[10] He challenged official religious rhetoric, bombastic public prayers, and the insidious way that the rich and powerful use religion to bless whatever it is they are up to. Despite what some on the Religious Right and others in the power-of-positive-thinking megachurch movement have done to the Gospel, it has never had anything to do with how to get rich. There are, however, numerous warnings about the futility of serving two masters and forgetting that compassion is what marks the truly religious human being.

By constantly using the word *evil*, Bush is only doing what fundamentalists of every stripe have done for centuries—demonizing first what you can exterminate later. If you can turn the Prince of Peace into a warrior and preach that your chosen war for the chosen people is approved by God in order to protect a chosen way of life, then you can justify all wars. But only if you *silence the prophetic tradition*.

By launching an unnecessary and disastrous war and causing the deaths of countless thousands, George W. Bush has turned the essential religious disposition upside down, driving a stake through the heart of every religious tradition's fervent prayers for peace. At their center, peace is the singular obsession of all religions. Every saint has lamented war and called on us to wage peace. Each regards violence as a form of separation from God. All have asked the question, in one form or another, if every war is fought "to end all wars," then why is it that war never ends?

To make matters worse, the rhetoric of the Christian Right, which often distorts the views of some evangelicals, condemns both the faith and the patriotism of those who disagree with them. The message is as pervasive as our love affair with yellow ribbons: "real" Americans and "real" Christians support the troops and keep on shopping. In fact, many of us—more than they know but will soon realize—support the troops by wanting to *bring them home alive* and consider shopping to be a necessary but not a religious experience.

In the either-or world of the saved and the "left behind," the sanctified and the "heathen," the Bible believers and the "secular humanists," there seems to be no middle ground. That familiar bumper sticker inscribed AMERICA: LOVE IT OR LEAVE IT always left me feeling that there must be more than just two options. What if you love it so much that you want to fix what's wrong and make it better? That's how a true parent loves his or her child and how a true patriot loves his or her country.

Such simplistic thinking, such moral laziness, has preceded all the world's most hideous atrocities. Whether the Inquisition, the Crusades, or the murder of Matthew Shepard, the idea that God commands us to convert others to our way of thinking by any means necessary is a cardinal sin. To believe that the lives of others are not as important as our lives is the genesis of all cruelty and reflects our refusal to see the image of God in all people. "Truly I tell you, just as you did it to one of the least of these who are members of my family, you did it to me" (Matthew 25:40).

> When you live in a country that has established international
> rules for waging a just war, built the United Nations on your
> own soil to enforce them, and then arrogantly break the very
> rules you set down for the rest of the world, you are doing
> something immoral.

When the United States agreed to be the permanent home of the United Nations, it represented one of the truly hopeful moments of the twentieth century. Born out of the ashes of two world wars and dedicated to the idea that human slaughter is not inevitable when nations are talking to one another, the UN was a symbol of the possibility of peace. It was built to provide a forum that the modern world had never known—an international forum to establish universal standards for human rights and exert collective pressure on nations to solve their problems diplomatically instead of going to war.

The Right has hated it ever since. Under President Ronald Reagan, the United States began withholding dues and tried to "starve the beast," a term first coined by David Stockman, Reagan's budget director, and now championed by Grover Norquist. The term is most often applied to the federal deficit, which is allowed to explode in order to justify reduced spending, especially on social programs. Those who despise the UN, like Jesse Helms, took a similar approach, hoping to weaken the institution or force it to adopt our reforms by choking off its funding.

The John Birch Society (an ostensibly Christian organization whose purpose was to stop the spread of communism) has called for the United States to get out of the UN in countless billboard and newspaper ads and to stop sharing our divinely sanctioned power with two-bit dictatorships. The idea that America should participate in any forum that allows open dialogue, including criticism of the United States by other countries, is a violation of the unilateralism that the Radical Right believes is our manifest destiny. As

Senate Majority Leader Trent Lott (R-Miss.) once put it, we should not "subcontract" our foreign policy to the UN.[11]

Fundamentalists of all stripes love a bully pulpit but hate a round-table. Why share power when you are right and everyone else is wrong? Who needs dialogue when your monologue is sacrosanct? Why let false prophets into the room when you can bolt the door and preach to the choir? Or to put it in terms that any good John Bircher can relate to, why let Cuba, for God's sake, spew its propaganda on the banks of the East River when every single last soul on that God-forsaken Communist island is going to hell anyway?

True fundamentalists, whether in religion or in politics, have no interest in sharing power. They seize it and then exercise it on behalf of those who need to be controlled. To reach a consensus requires compromise, and compromise has a whiff of weakness about it. To the patriarchs of the Christian Right, the smell is distinctly feminine. Winner-take-all means giving up nothing. Real men don't do roundtables. They plop themselves down at the head of the table—which is ironic, given specific instruction by Jesus to do otherwise. He taught his followers to take the lowest seat and hope that someone might invite them to move up (Luke 12:7–11).

When Bush the Elder got ready to wage the first Gulf War and repel the invasion of Kuwait (a country essentially created by the West to control the flow of oil at the mouth of the Persian Gulf), he sought the backing of the United Nations and got it. According to the rules for waging war set down by the UN, Iraq's invasion of a sovereign country could be met with force under international law. Once the mission was completed, the president knew better than to go to Baghdad, because that exceeded the mission approved by the UN. It would also spell disaster, as he explained in a book that highlights the difference between father and son:

> We should not march into Baghdad. To occupy Iraq would instantly shatter our coalition, turning the whole Arab world against us and make a broken tyrant into a latter-day Arab hero. Assigning young

soldiers to a fruitless hunt for a securely entrenched dictator and condemning them to fight in what would be an unwinnable urban guerrilla war, it could only plunge that part of the world into ever greater instability.[12]

The elder Bush, an Episcopalian, seemed to look at the world in a more nuanced way, while the son's born-again approach favors a cosmic battle between good and evil. Besides, critics of the elder Bush had once called him a wimp, and for a son who lived in his father's shadow and suffered the loss of his younger sister, a kind of macho intransigence may have been a powerful way to differentiate himself from his dad. No one would ever call him a wimp. As for the Gospel's paradox of "finding strength in weakness," this is not a popular option in West Texas.

In the run-up to the war, the president's taunting and dismissive comments about the United Nations betrayed his impatience with anyone foolish enough not to agree with him. After all, who needs to share power when you are the world's only superpower? "Onward Christian Soldiers" means exactly that, and Bush reminded us all, again and again, that we did not need to get "a permission slip from France" to defend ourselves.

This anti-French sentiment worked well at first, even though it was childish and made American legislators who suggested renaming french fries "freedom fries" look ridiculous. But in the end, it was an international public relations disaster. After no weapons of mass destruction were found, no links to al-Qaeda, and no "imminent threat," we were found guilty only of blaming the French ambassador for being smart enough to oppose the war that we were stupid enough to start. Conservatives may dislike the French for other reasons (those funny-looking berets and those uppity women, for example), but they are not the "enemy" because they disagreed with our decision to invade a sovereign country in violation of international law.

Today's Christian Right, and the political Right that it legitimizes, lives by a double standard that is almost stupendous in its audacity. Rules are for other people to live by. Lies are what other people tell. Sex is what other people have. When confronted with the painful truth that the Democratic presidential candidate, John Kerry, was a bona fide war hero running against a privileged Texas playboy who was AWOL from the National Guard, these great defenders of Western moral values couldn't care less about "bearing false witness." Presidential adviser Karl Rove, although he makes no explicit claim to being a Christian, is the dark political genius behind the Bush political dynasty. The tactics he employs on behalf of a "Christian" president indict the whole administration. After all, what is Christian about character assassination? There is no biblical text that says, "If you don't like the message, smear the messenger."

All that matters in the end, however, is winning. Fundamentalists are "true believers"—in religion, politics, or both. They seem unconcerned by whether anything they say or do is logical or verifiable. From pretending that "intelligent design" is a scientific theory to pretending to care about the United Nations, it's all in a day's devotional. As George W. Bush made the case for going to war against Iraq, we got a glimpse into the way his mind works. To put it in the language of logic, he is unfazed by the fallacy known as a non sequitur: he repeatedly called on Saddam Hussein to stop ignoring UN resolutions while at the same time claiming that the United Nations itself was "irrelevant" for failing to authorize the invasion he had already decided to launch. That is, it was a crime for Hussein to ignore the UN but merely pathetic for the UN to ignore Bush!

The last time—the *only* time—that the United States went to the United Nations to accuse another nation of possessing weapons of mass destruction was in October 1962. In the face of skeptics and Soviet denials, Adlai Stevenson, the U.S. ambassador to the United Nations, presented unmistakable photographic evidence of nuclear missiles being constructed on Cuban soil. When French President Charles de Gaulle was asked if he wanted to see the photos that brought the world to the brink of nuclear war, he waved them off, saying, "No, no, no, no. The word of the President of the United States is good enough for me."[13]

Not anymore. With good reason, much of the world has now lost the trust that is essential to international diplomacy. Hypocrisy, after all, is a form of dishonesty. When the president quotes the United Nations Human Rights Commission on Iraqi violations, he conveniently forgets that the same commission has criticized the human rights records of American allies, only to have them summarily dismissed by U.S. officials. While repeatedly condemning Saddam Hussein for violating UN resolutions, Bush seems unaware that they do not begin to compare with the number of Security Council resolutions currently being violated by American allies, including the most extensive violator, Israel.[14]

There is no doubt, of course, that Saddam Hussein was playing games with the weapons inspectors and thumbing his nose at the UN. What is remarkable, however, is what we now know about how *effective* the UN was at containing Iraq. Even with all its imperfections, the UN was not only not "irrelevant" but managed through embargos and sanctions to isolate a tyrant we had once befriended and armed against Iran and virtually eliminated his ability to threaten his neighbors, much less the United States.

That's why the Bush approach to making war against Iraq left the United States looking like a hypocrite. If the Gospel's highest calling is to love the neighbor, then what are we to make of a professing Christian president who *dismisses* his neighbor? Faith is supposed to elevate the worthiness of the stranger and make us see the face of God in every human being. But this president sees his neighbors as servants, not as children of God. If they serve us properly, they are rewarded. But if they have a mind of their own, they are rebuked. If humility is a sure sign of faith, then what is petulance but a sure sign of its absence?

Building the United Nations was itself an act of faith. It was born out of the hope that together we could put obstacles in the way of nations that are tempted to act unilaterally. After the bloodiest century on record, the UN was determined to try to prevent nations from going to war against other nations that had not invaded them or any other nation. To do this, we established the Security Council to render judgments on the war rationales of its fellow nation-states. Bringing the war-making machinery of tyrants out of the darkness and into the light was the UN's most important mandate.

That's why it was particularly embarrassing, and a disaster in the eyes of the rest of the world, to have the UN's founding nation thumb its nose at the organization it had established for the express purpose of trying to keep other nations from doing exactly what it was about to do! Using the rhetoric of divine sanction and suggesting that nobody will protect us if we don't protect ourselves, Bush proved that international rules are fine when they work in our favor but "quaint" when they don't. In so doing, he disgraced the office by taunting those who disagreed with him and suggesting that the UN is relevant only when it follows his lead.

Forever preaching to the world about "freedom" and "liberty" and the "march of progress" that God desires for every last human being despite the best efforts of the "evildoers who hate freedom," Bush acts as if we own the franchise on such virtues and that we alone know what is best for other nations, even if they don't know what's best for themselves. Such arrogance is the antithesis of faith and brings to mind a text that is surely familiar to him: "Why do you see the speck in your neighbor's eye but do not notice the log in your own eye?" (Matthew 7:3).

Chapter Two

Missing in Action:
The Sermon on the Mount

> When you claim that Jesus is the Lord of your life and yet fail to
> acknowledge that your policies ignore his essential teaching
> or turn them on their head (you know, Sermon on the Mount
> stuff like never returning violence for violence and those who
> live by the sword shall die by the sword), you are doing some-
> thing immoral.

If the church is to be saved, it will be have to be *recovered*. By this
I don't mean to say that we can turn back the clock to some nostal-
gic, nonexistent moment when everyone agreed on the nature of
God, sin, and salvation but rather to a time when membership in
The Way required no creeds and only one simple confession: *Jesus
Christ is Lord*.

Impossible as it seems today, when so many defenders of the faith
stake out theological positions and then defend them like a gun-
fighter, the essence of the Christian faith did not begin as a set of beliefs *about* Jesus but as response *to* Jesus. The first followers were not
part of a school of thought but a beloved community, formed in response to a beloved teacher who opened the heavens and revealed a
God whose unconditional love astonished them. It was a God they
had never met, revealed by a man they could never forget.

The early Christians did not blend into the culture but defied
it, living simply, regarding their neighbors as equals in the eyes of

God, ceasing the practice of animal sacrifice, and caring for one another as if each and every human being was in fact Jesus himself,
incognito. At its birth, Christianity was *relational*, not dogmatic.
Meeting underground in locations marked with the sign of the fish,
early Christians risked their lives to worship because they no longer
feared death. Possessed of a kind of radiance that astonished those
who beheld it, they practiced radical mutual regard and seemed to
have discovered the secret of happiness. One of the earliest obser-
vations on record from an outsider is this: "See how these Christians love one another!"[1]

Nobody put the case for this more forcefully that the author of
1 John: "We love because he first loved us. Those who say, 'I love
God,' and hate their brothers or sisters, are liars; for those who do
not love a brother or sister whom they have seen, cannot love God
whom they have not seen. The commandment we have from him
is this: those who love God must love their brothers and sisters also"
(4:19–21).

Although it did not take long for disagreements to arise, the first
disciples were not held together by the creeds of the third and fourth
centuries, as most Christians now claim to be, but by a new, first-
century way of being in the world. It is this distinctive way of being
that we will have to recover if the church is to survive. The disconnect
now between what people *say* they believe and how they actually *be-
have* has become untenable to the point of absurdity. We can survive
our disagreements over doctrine in the church; we always have. But
we cannot survive giving lip service to Jesus of Nazareth and then acting as if he taught nothing and wanted fans instead of followers.

Anyone who has ever served on a church committee or tried to
balance a budget knows that we often avoid the really important
work of the church by arguing over the most trivial things. Perhaps
it is to avoid facing the screaming pain of the world or the broken
lives around and among us that we threaten to walk out if the par-
lor is painted the wrong color or the youth group gets to eat pizza
on the new carpet. It could be, as one noted preacher put it, that
the principal heresy of the church in our time is *silliness*.[2]

But I suspect that the frustration now runs even deeper than the games people play or the ways that they deny what really matters. Some of the best and brightest human beings alive today have run screaming out of the sanctuaries where they went looking for spiritual nourishment and a chance to serve God for an even more insidious reason: *they miss Christianity.*

It's not just that they are frustrated by the dickering over decor or arguments about how many angels can dance on the head of a pin. After all, the church is made up of fallible human beings. The problem is deeper and much more disturbing. At precisely the moment in history when the qualities of authentic faith are most desperately needed, they are wondering, *what happened to the Gospel?* Not what does it really mean, but where on earth has it gone?

During the 2004 presidential campaign, which may go down in history as the most childish and trivial campaign ever, the party that most identified itself with traditional Christianity could not even be counted on to act *decently,* much less graciously. Those who were campaigning to "restore" religion to the land and crusading against secular humanists looked a lot more frightening than the secular humanists! In many cases, thoughtful people wondered aloud if becoming a believer made a person better or just meaner.

Yet somehow, despite it all, the hunger for the return of the Prodigal Jesus has also taken hold of those people who do not want to give up the soul of Christianity without a fight. A kind of underground movement of discontent is being born, aided by the Internet and fashioned after a kind of spiritual Woodstock—as if people everywhere are suddenly aware that Jesus has become a missing person.

Sometimes, in fact, I have this disturbing dream set to the tune of Melanie Safka's "Look What They've Done to My Song, Ma." Just before waking, when morning slumber has stripped away the superego and the id rises in the form of disturbing images, I find myself in back of some grand cathedral where I hear noises coming from the janitor's closet. The noises sound desperate, but nobody is listening. Instead, I see a splendid procession of adorned clerics going up the center aisle singing "The Church's One Foundation."

As the preacher begins his sermon, opining on the subject of "knock and the door will be opened to you," the banging and babbling from the broom closet grows louder. Upon opening it, I see Jesus standing there—the Jesus of history, the central figure of human history, the radical teacher who comforted the afflicted and afflicted the comfortable. He has been tied up and muzzled with duct tape!

When I tear off the piece that stretches across his mouth, the first words that come out are these: "Not everyone who says 'Lord, Lord' will enter the kingdom of heaven, but only the one who does the will of my Father in Heaven" (Matthew 7:21).

Is this really just a bad dream, or is it a description of the times in which we live? Every day, the so-called Christian Right tells us that the decline of morality in our time is the result of the "enemies" of morality: the Supreme Court ruling against mandatory prayer in public schools, the rise of rock and roll, the hostility of our culture toward religious symbols in the public square. But I think the true enemies of religion are *inside* the door, not outside it.

The recent effort by Alabama judge Roy Moore to have a three-ton monument of the Ten Commandments left on display in his courtroom is a perfect example of why the Christian Right is all heat and no light.[3] Not only did he violate the law he took an oath to defend (breaking the commandments about not breaking oaths and bearing false witness), but he also created a traveling shrine of the culture wars (breaking the commandment against idolatry and the making of graven images).

As the monument is wheeled around the country and Judge Moore gives speeches to boost his own plans for public office, very angry people come in the name of Jesus to pray, to weep, and to curse the darkness. America is a Christian nation, they believe, and any government that would remove this icon of "moral clarity" from the very place where those who break the law must receive swift and sure punishment has opened the door to moral relativism and forgotten that God did not give us the Ten Suggestions.

With all due respect to the Ten Commandments, and all that is both wise and misunderstood about them, why are followers of Jesus so intent on the public display of a document from the Hebrew Scriptures? They were obviously important to Jesus, but when asked by the rich young ruler which of the commandments he should follow to inherit eternal life, Jesus gives only *six* commandments, all related to religious *behaviors*: you shall not murder; you shall not commit adultery; you shall not steal; you shall not bear false witness. Honor your father and mother. And you shall love your neighbor as yourself (Matthew 19:18b–19).

Notice that the four commandments he leaves out are all specifically related to formal religious *observances*: "You shall have no other gods before me. You shall not make for yourselves an idol. You shall not make wrong use of the name of the Lord your God. Remember the Sabbath Day, and keep it holy." This is no small difference. Not only does Jesus *edit* the Ten Commandments (which sounds like "moral relativism" to me), but he lists only those that are *universal* rather than particular religious principles.

The six commandments of Jesus could actually hang anywhere without violating the separation of church and state, because they are part of the religious teachings of every world religion. They all have to do with how one treats the "other" (don't murder the other, don't commit adultery against the other, don't steal from the other, don't lie to the other, honor those very special others who gave you life, and love the other as yourself). The omitted commandments, on the other hand, have to do with how one honors a particular religious tradition (I am the one God, don't substitute idols for Me, don't misuse my Name, and remember to worship Me on the Sabbath). It is rather amazing to consider that the six commandments of Jesus don't mention God or faith but are consistent with all his teachings about religion as compassion, not allegiance. By the time the Gospel of John is written, his list of commandments is down to one: "I give you a new commandment, that you love one another" (13:34).

Although Jesus expressly reminded his followers that he had not come to destroy the law but to complete it, he did give us a "new covenant," which by definition is meant to supersede the old one. Whether he was consciously trying to found a new religion, which is doubtful, he offered such a striking departure from established religious ideas that his followers literally "took their leave" from the religious ethos of their time. They stopped practicing animal sacrifice, believing that with the death and resurrection of Jesus it was no longer necessary to appease God or seek atonement through blood. Marked by radical inclusiveness, an open table, and the elevation of the last and the least, The Way was born, and eventually a divorce from Judaism as well.[4]

This begs an obvious question, however: Why is the Christian Right more concerned with selective legal aspects of the Old Testament than with the heart and soul of the New Testament? In particular, why is nobody demanding that the Sermon on the Mount be made into a monument and placed in courtrooms and school buildings throughout the land? Why are followers of Jesus not weeping and praying over the eight beatitudes or cursing the darkness of a commander in chief who taunts our enemies instead of praying for them?

Could it be that the political agenda of the Christian Right is better served by the very image of God that Jesus rejected? Could it be that many conservative Christians find the old images of God as Lawgiver and Judge to be more appealing in these frightening times than the "kinder, gentler" Jesus of the Sermon on the Mount? The Ten Commandments, after all, draw a bright line in the moral sand and seem to represent the kind of "moral clarity" that so many believe could restore the nation, straighten out our kids, save our marriages, and give lenient judges the biblical rod they need to avoid spoiling the child of the criminal class.

The Sermon on the Mount is the Constitution of the Christian faith. The fifth, sixth, and seventh chapters of Matthew would, if taken seriously, turn the world upside down—especially our world. The world of power, privilege, ego, vanity, and greed. A world that encourages conspicuous consumption and a shameful disregard for both the environment and people in need. A world of entitlement thinking in search of religious sanction. A world drunk on its own righteousness, blind to the goodness in others, and quick to blame the poor for being poor. A world where fear stands in for love, the chosen are called to circle the wagons, and the big stick has replaced the "still, small voice."

The Big Lie in the church today is that calling on the name of Jesus justifies whatever it is that one is up to. The sad state of a nation where 82 percent of the population claims to be Christian is that the faith we say we cherish was born to resist the notion of divinely sanctioned empire. From the beginning, being a Christian meant saying yes to Jesus, the anti-Caesar, and no to the ways of Rome. Yet now we are the colossus astride the world, subduing all who dare to challenge us and striking fear in the hearts of those who might. When you have a hammer in your hand, everything looks like a nail.

At the heart of our national dilemma is the paradox of the Gospel itself. Either God's power truly is "made perfect in weakness," or that's just a clever but useless religious idea in a big, bad world. Either we mean it when we say that violence is a downward spiral or we just like the sound of it in church. Either mercy is truly right, and not might, or it's the harmless stuff of Sunday school. But we can't have it both ways. We can't take the Gospel for a joyride on Saturday night and then talk about how much we will respect her in the morning.

America is going fascist, and it's doing so with the help of religious zealots whose real passion is for the politics of privilege, not the radically disturbing presence of Jesus. This will sound alarmist to some, but the truth is that no country ever thinks it is going fascist until it wakes up one day to that indisputable reality. Then the people will say, "How did this happen?" And the answer is "one day at a time, and with the blessing of the church."

Many will say that we are angry because we are apologists for the Democratic Party. But the truth is, many committed lifelong Republicans are now as disillusioned as anyone. Besides, the timidity and impotence of today's Democrats in the face of Republican wrongdoing is enough to make them accessories to the crime. At just the moment when we needed principled and courageous *leaders*, we got only politicians. Instead of speaking truth to power, which is a sacred responsibility, no one "took up a cross" without first reading the poll numbers.

If we have such high regard for a penniless rabbi who went willingly to his own death rather than take back a single word of his blessed truth, then what are we to make of leaders who say they love Jesus but don't regard the truth as something to tell but rather as something to "spin." Not all of us who disagree with the president are trying to act like mad prophets decrying the hypocrisies of our time. We lodge our protest in the name of a faith we believe has been hijacked and on behalf of a country we love but hardly recognize anymore.

It is not just a set of political ideas that we oppose but the religious pretensions that accompany the way those policies are packaged and sold. You can't just wave incense over greed and then call it a virtue. You can't enrich the already rich and take milk out of the mouths of babes and then say how much you love Jesus. If you are going to dare to call yourself a Christian, then you do not have the option to make up the Gospel as you go. The Gospel is an inheritance. It comes as a gift and a demand. It is not an instrument of power, like political clay, but a subversive agent of conscience—like the angel that wrestled with Jacob by the banks of the Jabbok River.

More than comfort in times of trouble, God is also a divine Adversary, wounding us before transforming us. Jacob's cry is telling: "I will not let you go until you bless me." When the sun comes up, he is limping and has a new name. Now we have it exactly backward. Without a struggle, we seek a blessing. Without being wounded, we ask to be made new. Our cry is the essence of cheap grace: "I will not bless You until You let me go."

I would have far more respect for today's political operatives if they pursued their vision of *Pax Americana* and left Jesus out of it. But the truth is, the political Right could not resist tapping into the deep resentments of the Christian Right. They share a similar passion for condemnation and the politics of fear. They know the power of a common enemy and so joined forces to pursue what they thought was a common agenda. In truth, the political Right was often more interested in votes than in faith-based reforms and ultimately pursued legislation that had little to do with religion and everything to do with wealth and power.

Instead of claiming, as Bush once did, that Jesus is the most important philosopher in his life (an answer that many suspect conveniently saved the president from admitting that he couldn't name any other philosophers), he should just come clean with his regrets. He should say that he has read Machiavelli and he has read the Sermon on the Mount, and as much as he admires the Nazarene, it's a dangerous world, and "as for me and my house, we will follow Machiavelli."

Otherwise, he is pretending to believe what he does not practice—and that is the scourge of Christendom. If George W. Bush were to read the fifth chapter of Matthew and then consider his own addiction to power and privilege, he would be undone. The beatitudes bless those who are powerless but worthy, while Bush promotes those who are powerful but worthless. His largest single campaign contributor in the 2000 election was Enron's Ken Lay, and the corporate crime wave that unfolded under this administration's watch cost countless Americans their pensions and their trust. The system has become so corrupt and freewheeling that it looks for all the world like open season on the "meek." They may inherit the earth, according to Jesus, but "not the mineral rights," as J. Paul Getty famously said.[5] As for tax cuts, they would be wasted on the meek. Nonmeekness will "trickle down."

"All presidents are in a bubble," said *New York Times* columnist Maureen Dowd, "but the boy king was so insulated he was in a thermos."[6] The disconnect is even more painful when you consider that the boy king claimed to have been tutored by Jesus. In the Sermon on the Mount, the Lord compares his disciples to salt and light, working their transformation quietly from within. Bush calls his method of transforming the world after his own image "shock and awe," which is perhaps the most egregious misuse of religious imagery in our time. The "wolf" that is a bombing campaign, pure and simple, has been dressed up in sheep's clothing by the Pentagon's noble naming machine. We don't really just go to war anymore; we simply perform "operations" for the good of the "afflicted." Whether it's "Desert Storm" or "Enduring Freedom," war is branded now, like an SUV. Never mind that Jesus said, "Let your speech be a simple yes or no."

If I may go on quoting Jesus in the Sermon on the Mount, it gets worse. The Lord counsels us to know the danger of anger and to reconcile our grievances with our enemies in person before offering our gifts to God. Bush orders young men and women into battle to settle old family scores or to prove that he is not his father while steadfastly refusing to meet with the mother of a dead soldier camped outside his Texas ranch.

Jesus cuts through the hypocrisies of adultery and divorce and reminds us that we had best be humble and not self-righteous. Bush ascends to the presidential throne by contrasting his virtue with his predecessor's sin and suggests that he alone can restore dignity and integrity to a sullied Oval Office. The Lord says do not swear sacred oaths but be honest and straightforward in what you say. There are now entire Web sites devoted to exposing the lies told by this born-again president, from the imminent insolvency of Social Security to the imminent threat of a nuclear Iraq.

The Lord warns us against retaliation, turning "an eye for an eye" on its head. Bush talks like a Texas sheriff and brags that he will find Osama bin Laden, "dead or alive." As to turning the other cheek, offering up more than is requested, going the second mile, and giving to everyone who begs from you, the president would call it socialism and unbefitting a self-made man like himself.

But in no respect has the heart of the Gospel been thrown to the wolves like our failure to challenge this administration's foreign policy with the counsel of Jesus to love our enemies and pray for those who persecute us. While no one is suggesting that we not protect ourselves, it would seem at least nominally Christian to give others the benefit of the doubt, rather than calling them the "axis of evil." Lack of engagement and dialogue, whether in North Korea or the Middle East, accomplishes nothing but the deepening of suspicion and hostility. Besides, the advice of the president's preeminent philosopher was always tipped in favor of reconciliation before worship: "So when you are offering your gift at the altar, if you remember that your brother or sister has something against you, leave your gift there before the altar and go; first be reconciled to your brother or sister, and then come and offer your gift" (Matthew 5:23–24).

In some ways, the Sermon on the Mount has not just been ignored but *reversed*. When the president claims that our enemies do not value human life or freedom and thus implies that they are beyond redemption, he is really saying that they deserve the death that we are dealing them. Anyone can love their neighbor and hate their enemy, Jesus teaches us. But his disciples love their enemies and not just their own brothers and sisters.

As for prayer breakfasts and consorting with big-name televangelists, Bush can't say he hasn't been warned: "Beware of practicing your piety before others in order to be seen by them; for then you have no reward from your Father in heaven" (Matthew 6:1). As for giving alms and praying, Jesus says that should be done in secret, not as a road show for a political constituency or as forced exercise in a public school. As for the futility of storing up treasures on earth and serving both God and wealth, George W. Bush has done more to enrich the already rich than any other American president.

When the president courts the evangelical vote, as he did once by accepting an invitation to speak at Calvin College, he is sometimes shocked to discover that there are evangelicals who no longer believe that he speaks for them or represents their faith. More and more professing Christians are beginning to ask themselves whether this is a meaningful model of conversion or a dangerous forgery. It is not enough, after all, to just talk constantly about the importance of Jesus in one's life and not expect someone to ask, so how has Jesus *changed* your view of the world, of the poor, of your enemy? To claim that Jesus is the most important "philosopher" in one's life is to assume that Jesus actually *has* a philosophy. What does Bush think it is? If you call that philosopher "Lord," then you have moved beyond the realm of ideas and into the realm of obligation.

Whatever else one might think about Jesus of Nazareth, he is surely more than just a form of neutral energy. He is not just some automotive additive, like STP, that you add to your tank in order to get wherever it is you are going faster and with fewer knocks. He would be much more interested in where you are going, and why. Whatever it is that religion is supposed to do to people, it is not supposed to leave them as it found them. Whatever it means to say that you believe in God, it has to mean more than the two of you winking at each other.

> When you act as if the lives of Iraqi civilians are not as impor-
> tant as the lives of American soldiers and refuse to even count
> them, you are doing something immoral.

The sad truth is, we don't know how many we have killed, and we never will know. That job is left to outside organizations who try to calculate the dead and do so at great risk. But why is it, when we are constantly told of the miraculous things that the "world's most advanced fighting force" can do, that we can't even count the number of innocent men, women, and children that we have killed? Two reasons: (1) we don't want the world to know, and (2) they are brown people who speak a strange language and worship what evangelist Franklin Graham calls a "different God."[7] We don't count them because they are not "us." They are "them."

One of the most important psychological prerequisites for war is that the enemy be made to seem less than human. One of the most important prerequisites for religious faith is that every single human being be seen as fully human—precious, sacred, a child of God. This makes war and faith incompatible at the most basic level, of course, but it makes an *unnecessary* war into a cardinal sin.

In basic training, all soldiers must be conditioned to kill other human beings because it does not come naturally. To do this, the enemy is dehumanized by being made into a object of disgust, primarily through language. Our adversaries are given names that denigrate them and make them part of a subhuman class. The Jews were "vermin" to the Nazis, and the Nazis were "Krauts" and "Jerries" to the Allies. The Japanese were "Japs," "Gooks," and "Slant Eyes." The enemy is demonized so that it can then be eliminated. Who objects, after all, to the eradication of "vermin"?

There are moments, however, when the illusions of warfare break down. In World War II, when American GIs were going through the personal effects of a slain enemy solider, they would often find more than they bargained for. In addition to securing his weapon, they would go through the soldier's personal belongings only to discover that he was not subhuman at all. In his wallet were pictures of a wife and children, smiling and eager for his return. They looked exactly like the pictures that our soldiers carried into battle, the kind they retrieved at the darkest hours, fingered for good luck, whispered to, kissed.

Then there were the names: real names like Hans, Otto, Hilda, Frieda—names given to real children who loved their real fathers and prayed real prayers at their bedside. At school, they sang patriotic hymns and waved little flags and believed that God was on their side. Perhaps there was a love note recovered or a fragment of verse or just a receipt from the cleaners. The realization at such moments was as painful as it was enlightening: This was not something expendable. This was someone just like me.

Don't the human beings that we are killing in Iraq at least deserve to be counted? If we don't count them or even attempt to count them, what are we saying? Officially, of course, we say, "We regret civilian casualties, and we do everything we can to avoid them" (except not going to war in the first place). But in every war, we are reminded, there is "collateral damage."

Surely this is the most insidious euphemism ever devised by the Pentagon, referring to the innocent dead as "collateral damage." It is much more palatable, of course, than "innocent women and children caught in the crossfire and blown to bits," but then why do we need to be shielded from the horror of a war that is being fought in our name with our money? We would rather not think about it at all, of course, but this is precisely why we must never be allowed to forget what war is and what war does.

When a major television network recently decided not to show *Saving Private Ryan*, ostensibly because of concerns for adult language and violence, many people believed that it was also a political decision in the face of declining support for the war (after all, it had already aired, unedited, twice, to commemorate Veterans Day 2001 and 2002). That movie, which some observers consider the most antiwar, pro-soldier movie ever made, opens with a scene so nauseatingly real that the audience feels as if it is actually storming the beaches of Normandy, submerged in the blood-red water, facing a rain of bullets, and wading through the terror and indiscriminate carnage that is war.

Even so, we have long been asked to accept the horror of soldiers killing other soldiers who are, after all, in the business of killing—but the death of civilians is the deepest shame of war and its final insanity. They are not, in fact, "collateral damage." They are girls and boys, moms and dads, brothers and sisters, aunts and uncles. They are the neighbor.

The expression "collateral damage" gets its meaning from the world of banking, of course, where collateral is something one must offer up in order to get something else that one wants. But then, in today's military doublespeak, nobody really "kills" anyone anymore. The word *kill* has long been retired from the military lexicon. Now we "neutralize" or "eliminate with extreme prejudice."

When Great Britain suffered its first wave of terrorist attacks on the subway, one of the young men acquainted with one of the suicide bombers was talking with a reporter about how anyone could do such a horrible thing. In searching for an explanation, he remembered something that his friend had said only days before making himself into a human bomb. "Why are there never any moments of silence for Iraqi children?"

This ever-escalating cycle of violence, where the deaths of innocents are avenged by the deaths of more innocents, is like staring into the abyss. Suicide bombers are not only deluded by visions of martyrdom and encouraged by those who distort Islam but represent yet another form of collateral damage. They are the orphans of hatred, who then sow the seeds of the very hatred they despise.

Our response to suicide bombers is perhaps the most important test of genuine religious faith in our time. When the president uses the latest suicide bombing as proof that the enemy is incomprehensibly, irredeemably evil, he actually helps fuel the very evil he deplores. The difference between the rhetoric of British Prime Minister Tony Blair and George W. Bush following a suicide bombing is not only instructive but also has enormous religious implications. Blair uses the rhetoric of his long-ago predecessor Winston Churchill to express resolve and the vision of an eventual victory over terrorism because the actions of a few will not unravel the resolve of the rest of us to be civilized.

Bush's rhetoric is essentially, "See, I told you so. This is what we're up against." In a typical response to a terrorist attack, the president always falls back on "us versus them." Speaking after the London transit bombings, he said, "The contrast couldn't be clearer between the intentions . . . of those who care deeply about human rights and human liberty and those who kill, those who've got such evil in the their hearts that they will take the lives of innocent folks."[8]

One need not have an ounce of sympathy for suicide bombers to know that this is a sure way to produce even more of them. What's more, when we claim to "care deeply about human rights," it may not persuade those who have seen the pictures from the prison at Abu Ghraib or watched the dismantling of the American system of justice at Guantanamo Bay. In the end, these self-righteous pronouncements are being made by the leader of an occupying army that has caused the deaths of tens of thousands of innocent Iraqis. We exploit innocence for political gain but fail to see that we too are killing countless "innocent folks."

It may be more comforting to think that suicide bombers are simply lunatics who have been promised virginal harems in heaven, but the truth may be as painful as it is elusive: this is, for some, the chosen method of fighting the occupation of Muslim lands by people whom they consider infidels and interlopers. We can use the term *innocent* to describe only the deaths of our own citizens or those killed by Iraqi "insurgents." But the terrorists don't see it that way, and the result is an endless cycle of violence.

The only hope we have now is to break the cycle of violence, not ramp it up with evildoer rhetoric. Every act of carnage throws us back onto the essential religious question, how is violence to be answered—with justice or with vengeance? Worldwide terrorism has increased dramatically since the invasion of Iraq, which is now being waged, we are told, to keep us safe from terrorism. It's not working. Bob Herbert of the *New York Times* compared it to "a constant spray of gasoline on the fire of global terrorism."[9]

Failing to count the innocents we have killed will be excused as a logistical matter, a diversion of vital military energy, and an impossibility to do accurately. But the signal it sends is devastating. In the public mind, what isn't counted doesn't count. Collateral damage becomes a mass grave in the mind's eye, easier to deal with than names, faces, and families. Besides, our religious leaders have made it clear that the enemy worships the Wrong God, and thus deserves to feel the wrath of those who worship the Right One.

Now we are living in a time of maddening and deadly myths, undergirded by perversions of religion on both sides. Here are three of the deadliest lies that we are asked to believe every day: (1) The war on terror we are waging has made us safer. (2) Our enemies' behavior is not a response to our actions but incremental proof that they hate our freedom and are hopelessly evil. (3) Pulling back from or changing this disastrous course would be an admission that we were wrong and that our soldiers have died in vain.

So this is our answer. This is the logic of our time: it is better to go on killing more of them, even if they go on killing more of us, so that we can remind everyone how vital it is that we kill more of them first.

It all reminds me of the shortest verse in the New Testament: "Jesus wept" (John 11:35).

Chapter Three

Rich Chicken Hawks for Jesus

When you find a way to avoid combat in Vietnam and then question the patriotism of someone who volunteered to fight and came home a hero, you are doing something immoral.

There is a name for men who send others off to war but avoid combat themselves. We call them "chicken hawks." They talk in misty-eyed platitudes about the heroism and nobility of "our troops," but they make sure that the bullets are flying far from their heads and that none of their children are ever in harm's way.

A chicken hawk loves to surround himself with soldiers and often dresses up like one. In fact, he seems to idolize soldiers, even though he did what he could to avoid becoming one. In the case of George W. Bush, like so many other men of the Vietnam generation, the preferred method of avoiding combat while still appearing to be patriotic was to hide out in the National Guard. Dan Quayle did the same thing and became both the vice president and a chicken hawk himself.

The defenders of Bush will be quick to point out, of course, that Clinton did not serve in Vietnam and yet sent troops to Bosnia. Is he a chicken hawk? That depends on whether you equate the humanitarian mission to stop genocide in the Balkans with the war in Afghanistan and the invasion of Iraq. It also depends on whether you think that Clinton, with his obvious reservations about the military, would ever have dressed up as a fighter pilot and landed on the deck of an aircraft carrier as a publicity stunt.

There was nothing unusual, of course, about trying to stay out of Vietnam in those days. Millions of us, myself included, did what we could to avoid that tragic war. The difference was the draft, which exposed the sons of the rich and the sons of the poor to the same lottery. Now we recruit soldiers with promises of money for college and the "adventure of a lifetime" in exotic ports of call. While they fight for us, almost like a mercenary army drawn from the young and the restless poor, the children of wealth and privilege never have to worry. War is now "outsourced," like everything else.

The potential dangers of so-called standing armies, made up of paid volunteers, instead of citizen armies drawn into compulsory service from across the socioeconomic spectrum, has been noted by everyone from Aristotle to Samuel Adams. Today's all-volunteer army, drawn heavily from the ranks of the poor and the middle class, is just such a standing army. Lean, mean, and high-tech, today's active-duty military can wage war while putting very few of America's privileged sons and daughters at risk. As Stanford professor David Kennedy put it, "Modern warfare lays no significant burdens on the larger body of citizens in whose name war is being waged."[1]

In fact, war has now become a choreographed and somewhat schizophrenic spectacle, just one more set of images like those we see in a video game. After the 9/11 attacks, when President Bush launched the bombing campaign against Afghanistan, he asked the American people for no sacrifices whatsoever. To the contrary, he is the first commander in chief ever to order soldiers into battle and citizens into the mall.

This unequal sacrifice betrays a fundamental religious principle that we bear one another's burdens and share one another's grief. When Jesus asks his disciples whether or not they are able to "drink the cup that I am about to drink, and be baptized with the baptism that I am baptized with" (Matthew 20:22), they said, "We are able." But he knows that they don't understand the difference between allegiance to an idea, and willingness to die for it. The critics who challenge the president to urge his own daughters to enlist are not just taking a cheap shot. They are alluding to the broader message of yet another passage, "Where your treasure is, there will your heart be also" (Luke 12:34).

More and more Americans have begun to realize that the most vociferous supporters of the war often do not back up that support by actually serving in the military. More Democrats than Republicans are war heroes, and few demographic groups have more vocal support but less actual enlistment than the Young Republicans.[2] While they disparage liberals for protesting the war, they believe they can best serve their country by going to college. There are elite business and law schools to attend and grand pronouncements to make about this being a "liberation," not a war. When asked why they are not doing the actual "liberating," these boisterous lads argue that their political work stateside is more important. That is, they march and cheer for Bush while poor and middle-class boys are literally dying to protect the lads' careers. From a distance, war is such a rush.

This raises an important dynamic of the chicken hawk. He is seldom willing to sacrifice personally for the freedom he so passionately espouses. Other people do the heavy lifting, and he cheers loudly from the sidelines. Some would argue that the president is a kind of chicken hawk Christian, not nearly as committed to the cause as the legions of true believers that surround him, but has merely co-opted the fears of a crucial voting bloc to assure himself a margin of victory. Either way, the public should be warned that this unholy alliance is about power, not intellectual or theological honesty. The president wears his faith on his sleeve, and because he surrounds himself with high-profile preachers who have delivered their constituency in exchange for his support, the agenda of the Christian Right and that of George W. Bush are perceived to be identical. Regardless of who is using whom, the message comes through loud and clear: this is the face of religion in our time. This is how a powerful born-again Christian looks, sounds, behaves.

Consider the means by which this administration sought to defeat John Kerry. It was an act of willful character assassination, and it was carried out by Republican operatives pretending to be "concerned Vietnam veterans." The Swift Boat Veterans for Truth proved that truth has nothing whatsoever to do with it. In fact, if your opponent has real credentials, it would make sense to change the subject, but not to Karl Rove. He has another idea: attack the credentials themselves. This will leave the impression that your opponent's strengths are really his weaknesses.

It has been said that the final act of grace is to make a person gracious. A gracious person knows that one's whole life is a blessing beyond deserving and that even those with whom one disagrees are possessed of dignity and deserving of respect. The test of a gracious human being is how he treats *other* humans beings, not how he uses them to seize power or elevate himself by comparison. Jesus did not say, "If you have a complaint against your brother, first destroy your brother."

The Bush family has a long history of political character assassination. The Bushes have achieved and held power not so much by being chosen as by being "left standing." In 1988, Lee Atwater, George H. W. Bush's presidential campaign manager, produced the most racist political ad ever to run on American television.[3] It featured the frightening black face of convicted murderer Willie Horton, who not only helped the elder Bush win the White House but proved that such overt appeals to a smoldering racism can be as powerful as the burning of crosses.

Because Horton was a convicted murder who killed again while out of prison on a weekend furlough from a Massachusetts prison, the message was as clear as it was fallacious: if Massachusetts Governor Michael Dukakis, the Democratic candidate, becomes president, our prisons will become revolving doors, and murderers will get weekend passes so they can rape and kill your wives and daughters.

Never mind that other states had similar furlough programs, including those run by Republican governors, and that similar crimes had been committed in those states as well. The face of Willie Horton had worked its dark magic. The world is a dangerous place, Republicans tell us again and again. Trust Daddy to protect you from all enemies, foreign or domestic.

Atwater was so full of guilt over producing that political ad that as he lay dying of a brain tumor, he apologized to the nation. That moment of remorse and genuine religious sentiment did not prove to be habit-forming. A new chief character assassin took over and raised the stakes of the game. It was Karl Rove who helped George W. Bush early in his career by starting a rumor that Texas Governor Ann Richards was a lesbian. Later, he planted the ideas that presidential candidate John McCain was mentally unstable and his wife was a drug addict.

It should come as no surprise to anyone, therefore, that the White House would be caught in a scandal involving the outing of CIA agent Valerie Plame. Her husband's op-ed piece in the *New York Times* disputing the administration's claim that Saddam Hussein had tried to acquire enriched uranium from Niger exposed the web of deceptions that led the country to war. After revealing her identity to punish and discredit her husband, the lying continued, as did the cover-up. It was business as usual for Karl Rove and company.

Don't like the message? Smear the messenger.

Yet the Bible that Bush keeps on his desk in the White House quotes one of the strongest and most straightforward of all the teachings of Jesus: "By your fruits you shall know them" (Matthew 7:20). So be it.

Onward Christian slander.

> When you ignore the fundamental teachings of the Gospels, which say that the way the strong treat the weak is the ultimate ethical test, by giving tax breaks to the wealthiest among us so that the strong will get stronger and the weak will get weaker, you are doing something immoral.

The twelve most radical words in the New Testament are those that begin the fifteenth chapter of Paul's letter to the Romans. If they were better known, they might be banned all the way from Washington, D.C., to Baghdad. But if the president wants to walk in the light of

Scripture, he might want to have these twelve words inscribed and hung over his desk in the Oval Office. In this case, they are at their most powerful in the old King James Version: "We who are strong ought to bear the infirmities of the weak."

Ernest Campbell, former minister of the Riverside Church of New York City, once preached a powerful sermon on those twelve words.[4] In it, he explained eloquently that the heart of the life of faith comes down to the way the strong treat the weak. This is the ultimate ethical test. Not the things we are told to believe about Jesus. Not the creeds of the fourth century. Not the soothing incantations of personal salvation. But how the strong use their strength on behalf of those who are not strong.

Indeed, Campbell reminds us, this is not some minor concern in Scripture. It is not some poorly marked trail down which Paul is wandering. It is more like "a six-lane expressway running through Scripture from start to finish." When Israel's religion was being tested, the questions were never theological; they were always *ethical*. The prophets never weighed in on various schools of thought or the latest rabbinical poll numbers. They were more interested in how people *acted* than in what they believed—especially when human beings were in need.

Their questions were aimed not at the head but at the heart. "How goes it in the land with the orphan, the widow, the stranger?" In other words, how are the strong treating the weak? Even the Ten Commandments, Campbell reminded us, could be thought of as God's way of trying to protect the weak: "Just because you're young, don't neglect your parents, honor them; just because you're strong and could do it, don't kill; just because you're good with words, don't hurt another with a lie; just because you're crafty and could get away with it, don't steal; just because you're attractive, don't move in on your neighbor's spouse."

This is how God puts the great arms of heaven around the weak ones in the world. Notice that the text does not say "*They* who are strong ought to bear the infirmities of the weak," for this is the language of uninvolved advice, says Campbell. It belongs to armchair generals, to tenured professors of economics, to social work bureaucrats who handled their last case twenty years ago, to politicians who are interested in divvying up everybody's wealth but their own.

Nor would the text mean anything if it said *"You* who are strong ought to bear the infirmities of the weak," for that is the language of confrontation, of political manifestos and revolutionary causes. The text gets its leverage, he says, because of the word *We*. *"We* who are strong ought to bear the infirmities of the weak." Take them on, ease them—not because we feel guilty or because we want to provide what is fashionably called a "social safety net" or because we fear that we might be weak ourselves someday, although this is profoundly true. Rather, we should do so simply because we are strong, and that strength is itself a gift.

Those of us who have, for whatever reason, power, wealth, influence, and talent ought to use those gifts on behalf of those who do not have them. When Hurricane Katrina swamped New Orleans and the Gulf Coast in unspeakable misery and death, the president's policies had already set the stage for a humanitarian disaster. The administration's blank check for the war and tax cuts for the rich had been paid for by cuts to vital social programs and a crumbling infrastructure.

We have the right to judge our presidents by how they respond to tragedy. It became painfully obvious that as he vacationed in Texas, Bush was simply oblivious to what was happening. I don't believe, as some people do, that he was motivated by malice. He just didn't have a clue. On the way back to Washington, he flew over the Gulf region in *Air Force One* and gazed down from the window in air-conditioned comfort for what would become a regrettable photo op. Here was the president, looking presidential, as he soared above the chaos and suffering below. Then he said, "It's devastating. It's got to be doubly devastating on the ground."[5]

That's where he should have been! The weakest of the weak were perishing, and the strongest of the strong did shamefully little. Perhaps he thought it was magnanimous simply to open the purse strings of the federal government after the fact, but what people needed was to see their president with his sleeves rolled up handing out food. Not to be politically correct but because the biblical ethic is deeper than quid pro quo. The Christian ethic is one of *consequence:* we love because we have already been loved. While we were yet abjectly weak, as Ernest Campbell put it, we were lifted out of our weakness and are now obligated to lift others out of theirs.

I have thought of that sermon many times over the years, but never so often as when listening to the current administration explain why it must cut taxes further for the wealthiest Americans. The answer is simple and turns Romans 15:1 on its head: the best way to help the poor, we are told, is to help the rich. We who are strong ought to help the strong get stronger.

Since 2001, the Bush administration, with the help of a devoutly religious House and Senate, have scaled back programs that help the poor in order to help pay for over $600 billion in tax breaks that benefit primarily the wealthiest Americans.[6] The meager tax savings for the poor and middle class have been more than swallowed up by state tax increases and user fees that local governments have been forced to adopt as the federal government swims in red ink. In many cases, the poor lost services and got no tax break at all!

The nonpartisan Congressional Budget Office reported that in 2004, the poorest 20 percent of workers (those earning $16,000 on average) got a tax break of $250, or less than 2 percent of their income, while the richest 1 percent (those earning over $1.1 million on average) received a tax cut of $74,460, or nearly 7 percent of their income. With Social Security rates rising nine times since 1979 to 6.2 percent but capped at $87,900, the lowest-paid workers pay the tax on all their income, while the richest 10 percent pay less than 2 percent of their income for Social Security. As more people slide into poverty in America, the Bush tax cuts put $148 billion into the pockets of the richest 10 percent of Americans in just one year.

We are told repeatedly that it will "trickle down," and some people continue to believe it, or pretend to, despite all the evidence to the contrary. Like snake oil salesmen, the Republican devotees of "supply-side economics" from Reagan onward have borne false witness to a failed economic theory to enrich themselves. Ironically, it was billionaire Ross Perot who told us the truth about supply-side economics. "In the 1980s," he is rumored to have quipped, "we threw lots of money at the top, and most of it stayed up there."

What must he be thinking now? During a time when the inequity of wealth was exploding and the middle class was struggling and even shrinking, the Republican Party of Jesus (a penniless rabbi from Nazareth who warned us that wealth could be spiritually debilitating) has reversed the lesson of the cleansing of the Temple. Instead of distancing themselves from the perversion of religion by money, the Republicans have used religious rationales to create more wealth and then explained it all as a sign of God's favor. It's called prosperity theology. The Gospel of the American dream. You can have all this and Jesus too.

Joel Osteen, the pastor of the country's largest church, with thirty thousand members regularly attending, recently bought the Compaq Center in Houston to accommodate the throngs of worshipers. The question is, what are they worshiping? The answer: mostly Osteen's advice to improve your attitude, think positive thoughts, let go of the past, and then expect God's blessings to rain down on you. Someone called it "cotton-candy theology," and it works. "Russell Conwell said it a century ago, Norman Vincent Peale said it fifty years ago, and Bruce Wilkinson said it with *The Prayer of Jabez* a few years back."[7] Nothing sells better than the Gospel wedded seamlessly to private ambition, and nothing is more contrary to the teachings of Jesus: "Do not store up for yourselves treasures on earth, where moth and rust consume and where thieves break in and steal; but store up for yourselves treasures in heaven, where neither moth nor rust consumes and where thieves do not break in and steal" (Matthew 6:19–20).

The issue here isn't whether positive thinking is good for you but rather what it has to do with being Christian. The emphasis of prosperity theology is on what *we* do, not on what God has already done. Since one doesn't need God to think positive thoughts, God will help, but only if we choose to be happy, positive, and generous first. "This is not a gospel of grace, in which God acts in spite of our lack of faithfulness to redirect our wants. Instead this is a gospel of rewards in which God does nothing until we get our act together. In traditional theology, Protestant and Catholic alike, we can do nothing in and of ourselves to merit God's favor."[8]

If Americans don't understand prosperity theology, they will fail to understand how fundamentally the Gospel has been hijacked. Whereas the Gospel warns us about the inherent dangers of wealth, the smiling preachers of prosperity use God-talk and financial planning so interchangeably that they become a kind of ecclesiastical blur. "Getting right with God" has become synonymous with getting *rich* with God, and in a capitalistic, individualistic culture, this is pure magic.

As for churches moving into former sports arenas, the evolution is inevitable. Being in the right church is like being on the right team. Winners play here, and losers wish they did. Christians were once identified by their voluntary poverty and simple lifestyle. Now they are more apt to be affluent, neatly coiffed, and assembling in enormous, garish auditoriums.

Osteen likes to ask his congregation the really deep questions of life, like this actual query in a recent sermon: "Are you satisfied with that little house you're in? You shouldn't be. You should want the sort of mansion the Osteens live in."[9]

As to the relationship between the size of one's house and the depth of one's faith, I had forgotten just where that verse was in the Bible, so I went back to look it up. All I could find with regard to what a disciple needs in the way of personal possessions was rather surprising: "You received without payment; give without payment. Take no gold, or silver, or copper in your belts, no bag for your journey, or two tunics, or sandals, or a staff; for laborers deserve their food. . . . If anyone will not welcome you or listen to your words, shake off the dust from your feet as you leave that house or town" (Matthew 10: 8b–14).

That was Jesus, counseling an *itinerant* way of life, poor in things and rich in truth. How are we to square this with so much preaching that counsels an opulent way of life behind walled neighborhoods, rich in things and oblivious to the truth? Some megachurches do spend money on the poor, and there are some programs that mirror the teachings of Jesus, but they are the exception, not the rule. In the church, as in the nation, it's all about the *individual* now. We have abandoned any collective vision of dealing with poverty in favor of a rising tide that is supposed to float all boats. It should come as no surprise to anyone that we once declared a "war on poverty," only to surrender, and have now declared a war on closed markets and the union movement, only to increase poverty and swear that we will never surrender.

When George W. Bush was appointed president by the Supreme Court in 2000, he came into office as the most publicly religious candidate in U.S. history. He embraced leading TV evangelists, spoke of being born again, and did what he could to break down the wall between church and state. He did not, however, carefully read the Bible on which his personal faith was based or the words of the Savior who put a stop to his drinking. Had he done so, it would have been impossible for him to consistently side with the rich against the poor.

In his first three years as president, he pushed through three massive tax cuts, the most ever by any administration, and all of them were tipped in favor of the rich. The government came to the aid of those who needed it least while cutting programs for those who needed it most. Using the rhetoric of selfishness ("It's *your* money"), Bush could speak of Jesus at the morning prayer breakfast and then act on the wisdom of Ayn Rand in the afternoon. Instead of following the scriptural counsel to use one's strength on behalf of the weak, this administration tapped into the dark American penchant for blaming the poor for being poor and admiring the rich as if they were all self-made.

Now what you see and what you hear is *definitely* not what you get. After standing in the middle of Jackson Square in New Orleans for a photo op and a sound bite after Hurricane Katrina, the president admitted that poverty and racism were still haunting America and needed to be addressed. In what sounded like a willingness to spend more on behalf of the poor, his real priorities came out a few weeks later in the budget: *spend less*—billions less through massive cuts in social programs, especially food stamps. How do these politicians justify spending less for programs that help the very people they say they want to help? They must be fiscally responsible, considering the "unusual" expenses of rebuilding after the hurricane! Yet the amount of "savings" from cuts in social programs for the poor were more than offset by even more tax cuts for the wealthy. Now we have Robin Hood in reverse: the rich steal from the poor, and the proceeds trickle up.

Instead of "rendering unto Caesar what is Caesar's" and allowing the government to perform its vital function of checking ravenous greed and protecting those too weak to protect themselves, these neo-Christians have perpetuated the Reaganite myth that the government *itself* is evil and that the marketplace is holy. If left alone, Adam Smith's "invisible hand" will solve all the problems of life. Talk about a dangerous myth!

My experience is that the rich always seem to know what is best for the poor, in a paternal sort of way. They assume that the universe is dealing out just deserts to all God's children in a perfectly logical manner. Got poverty? Get busy and climb out of it. Need money for college? Go to the bank and borrow it. Too many hungry mouths to feed? Just say no.

Men of privilege talk about it at the country club, chewing on cigars and drinking martinis. Every time the subject of welfare comes up, they are all in perfect agreement. It creates dependence and leads to sloth, they say, as they order another round of drinks. Then come the inevitable jokes about Cadillacs and food stamps and lots of sentences beginning with the transparently absurd "Now I'm not prejudiced, but . . ."

Sometimes I have regretted staying at those tables too long and not getting up and walking out when I should have. Nothing is as un-Christian as the entitlement mentality, and yet it is epidemic these days. White males who woke up on third base and thought they hit a triple. Men who make money the "old-fashioned way"—they inherit it.

Years ago, when I was a minister in Detroit, my wife, Shawn, and I were invited to dine at the home of an executive in the Ford Motor Company. The house was palatial, the setting was ostentatious, and the conversation was almost unbearably phony. As the black maid shuffled back and forth between the kitchen and the table, no one spoke to her. We wondered if she had a name. If Mr. Executive wanted his plate taken away, he just waved his hand over it like a bored magician, and she would make it disappear.

For some reason, as we sipped our after-dinner drinks and our host spoke impatiently about all things inferior, the subject of Kent State University came up. Kent State is where four students had been slain by the National Guard during a rally protesting the Vietnam War. I referred to it as a "tragedy," and that word stopped this gilded man in mid-chew.

"A tragedy you say? Not so. If you ask me, those kids got exactly what they deserved."

It was the closest that I have ever come to choking before swallowing. For a moment, I thought he was joking. But then, in the silence that followed, I realized that he was serious. In his world, long-haired students were part of the expendable class. They were foul-mouthed and unkempt and hard on the flag, so off with their heads!

I should have reminded him that two of the students killed were not even part of the protest but were hit by stray bullets as they walked across campus to class. That's when I remembered the line from Neil's Young's song "Ohio," when "Soldiers are gunning us down. . . . / What if you knew her / And found her dead on the ground / How can you run when you know?"[10]

I have always been ashamed of myself for not getting up and leaving that table. But I was a young minister, new on the job, and he was on the board of trustees. Now I know what I should have done. I should have folded my napkin, pushed back that elegant chair, and said, "I'm sorry, but I am a Christian minister, and I have suddenly lost my appetite."

Trickle down? A culture of life? It's all a lie, and it's high time we said so.

> When you wink at the torture of prisoners and deprive so-
> called enemy combatants of the rules of the Geneva Conven-
> tion, which your own country helped establish and insists that
> other countries follow, you are doing something immoral.

Should America fall into the dustbin of history, another Promised Land impaled on the sword of empire, it will not take historians long to peg the moment we lost our soul. What will seem odd, however, is the Arabic name they will reference and the pornographic nature of what went on there. How did a country founded by grim-lipped Puritans end up exposing their own dark side so graphically while pretending to be the world's moral policeman? How could we claim to be so deeply religious and yet so mortally wound our own credibility? What does *Abu Ghraib* mean, anyway? And where is this place called Guantanamo Bay, which turns out to be an evil twin sister and the mother of lost souls?

Shortly after Bush declared war on terrorism, using the word *war* in a way that remains controversial even among his own administration, he met secretly to begin rewriting the rules for the American treatment of prisoners. The attacks of 9/11 were "an act of war," he said, and we are "a nation at war," he told us again and again. Against the advice of his own military leaders, who now understand that we are involved in a complicated and deadly worldwide struggle against a pathological hatred of the West, Bush continues to use the language of war to justify the USA PATRIOT Act, domestic wire tapping without a warrant, and the most disastrous changes to the treatment of prisoners in U.S. history.

During military sweeps in Afghanistan and Iraq, suspected terrorists, most of them innocent, were taken to a military compound at Guantanamo Bay, Cuba, and held without access to any legal counsel. They were not formally charged, were held indefinitely, and were tortured in ways that humiliated not only them but all Americans as well.

The administration claimed they were "enemy combatants" and therefore did not deserve the protections of the Geneva Convention. Attorney General Alberto Gonzales, in the now infamous "torture memo," called provisions of the Geneva Convention "quaint."[11] The administration successfully reinstated military tribunals and can now suspend the most basic standards of jurisprudence to secure the high-profile convictions it needs to prove that we are winning the "war" on terrorism. While gagging on the word *gulag*, it turns out that the CIA is alleged to have established secret prisons in eastern Europe, where it practices "rendition"—a euphemism for torture.

When photographs of the abuse of prisoners at Abu Ghraib were flashed around the world, including naked, hooded prisoners in sexually humiliating situations, some with wires attached to their genitals and others led around on leashes like dogs, the president did what he always does. He feigned indignation and called it an aberration, a "few bad apples." "This is not the America I know," he said, shaking his head.

The sad truth, however, which always lags far enough behind the headlines to disappear in the short attention span of the public, is that the torture of prisoners at Abu Ghraib was first tested at Guantanamo Bay. What's more, that those "bad apples" who took the fall only after it was caught on tape tried to tell the world repeatedly they were acting in ways already approved at the highest level of this supposedly Christian administration. America is now embroiled in a political debate about whether we should make torture legal.

In tactics approved by Defense Secretary Donald Rumsfeld and used months before they surfaced in photographs at Abu Ghraib, one stubborn detainee was forced to wear women's underwear and confronted with snarling dogs that were attached to his chains. Another was harassed by a female guard who pretended to confront a prisoner with her own menstrual blood and acted in sexually provocative ways on advice from a psychologist who argued that it would enrage his religious sensibilities. Reports of a Koran being flushed down the toilet could not be confirmed, but other methods of desecration were. The world began to make up its own mind about the president's claim that we "respect Islam and its followers."[12]

The truth is, before the soldiers started taking pictures, it was American military leaders who lodged the most vigorous complaints against the president's authority to order harsh interrogations of prisoners. It was military lawyers, not the American Civil Liberties Union, who warned the administration that some of the methods amounted to violations of domestic criminal law as well as military law. In response to these warnings, a task force concluded that military interrogators and their commanders would be immune from prosecution for torture under federal and international law. In this exalted ethic, it's not what you do that matters but what you can get away with.

So while some members of the military were baptizing prisoners in a washtub outside Baghdad to save them from the fires of hell, others were ordering them to form naked human pyramids and simulate sex acts. It would be hard to imagine anyone coming up with a worse idea for "winning the hearts and minds" of an Arab society where the major complaint against the "infidels" is that we speak out of both sides of our mouth.

Suddenly it seemed to everyone who could read and think that the United States had become a "law unto itself," as one Army lawyer put it, endangering our own soldiers in the future. But more than this, the torture of detainees by American forces betrayed our most basic values and mocked the idea that we are a deeply religious people. If the fundamental premise of our faith is summed up by the Latin phrase *imago Dei*, made in the image of God, then what on earth are we doing when we use humiliation as the principal means of breaking down other human beings?

Perhaps the most telling moment in this debate occurred on the floor of the Senate when three Republican senators tried to get the White House to change course on the cruel and degrading treatment of detainees. One of their own colleagues, Jeff Sessions (R-Ala.), defended the president because, he argued, the detainees are not prisoners of war but "terrorists." But it was Senator John McCain (R-Ariz.), a Vietnam War POW, who spoke truth to power. He said, "It's not about who *they* are. It's about who *we* are." Americans, said McCain, "hold ourselves" to a higher standard.

The situation has become so bad that three hawkish members of the president's own party find themselves arguing for more humane treatment of prisoners because they are dismayed at what this "pro-life, family values" administration is doing to the international reputation of the United States. As *New York Times* columnist Bob Herbert put it, the United States should "not just fight harder than its enemies, but also stand taller."[13] Franklin Pierce, a former admiral, put it more dramatically. He said that if we don't get our act together with regard to the humane treatment of detainees, we will "have changed the DNA of what it means to be an American."[14]

What an interesting way to put it. But perhaps we could extend the metaphor even further. If we don't exhibit a basic respect for the sacred in all living things, including our enemies (which is the real definition of "pro-life"), then we have done more than change the DNA structure of what it means to be an American. We have mangled it when it comes to being a Christian.

Chapter Four

Terminal False Dichotomies

When you claim that the world can be divided up into the good guys and the "evildoers," slice up your own nation into those who are with you or with the terrorists—and then launch a war that enriches your own friends and seizes control of the oil to which we are addicted instead of helping us kick the habit, you are doing something immoral.

There is a dangerous virus loose in the American cultural bloodstream, one that has gone largely unrecognized and untreated. It is spread largely through repeated contact with television, and the symptoms are most apparent on Fox News and in the logic of the average bumper sticker. The technical term for this epidemic is *media-induced terminal false dichotomies*, or MITFD. Unfortunately, the only effective treatment for MITFD is critical thinking. Otherwise, in a democracy, it can be fatal.

In addition to serving for two decades as the minister of Mayflower Congregational Church, I am also a professor of rhetoric in the philosophy department at Oklahoma City University. One of my responsibilities in that role is to offer an undergraduate class called Logic and Contemporary Rhetoric. It is an informal logic class that introduces students to the rules of cogent versus fallacious reasoning. The experience has been more than just a bit sobering. It has been downright frightening. Many college students these days have no idea how to think critically or even how to become self-conscious or self-critical about their own methods of reasoning. Hence they are often at a loss to explain why they believe the things they believe except to say that something is "just common sense" or that they were "raised right" or that other points of view are "just too weird."

Most students are chips off the old parental block—conservative students mirror their conservative upbringing, and liberal students do the same. But from time to time, a student will actually break the cycle and think independently. After all, the purpose of the university is to *disorient* students in order that they might *reorient* themselves.

The majority, however, often seem to fear new ideas lest they become confused. Once I was trying to explain to a student that even though I'm a minister and believe that Scripture is inspired, I don't believe it is inerrant or infallible. She looked at me, crestfallen, and said, "Why *can't* you believe that?"

I explained that I was aware that I *could* believe that but that careful study of the Scripture had persuaded me that I *shouldn't*. "Oh, yes," she said, "you should." That was the end of the conversation.

There seems to be a great and heated debate these days about why students should even go to college. As its turns out, a wise old Cherokee woman from Oklahoma came up with the answer a long time ago. She said to me once, "Robin, do you know why everyone should go to the university?"

"To get a good job?" I said.

"No," she continued. "People should go to college for the same reason that people empty from a crowded church more slowly."

Forgive the expression, but I was buffaloed. I looked at her blankly, and she continued, "Have you ever been in a church that wasn't very full?"

"Yes, I've even stood in front of a few," I said, attempting a little self-deprecating humor.

"Did you notice how quickly it emptied out after the service?"

"Well, yes," I said. "There's not much resistance."

"Exactly. But think about a crowded church. After the benediction, people exit a crowded church more slowly, don't they?"

"Well, yes, of course," I said. "More resistance."

"That's why people must go to the university. Before they go, they have only a few ideas, like a handful of worshipers in the nearly vacant sanctuary of their mind. When they open their mouths to speak, all they hear is their own echo—the sound of a lonely, unexamined thought. It falls out quickly and becomes an intellectual orphan in the parking lot."

I thought about this for a moment, and she continued.

"But when the mind is full of new ideas, competing voices, and different points of view, a person waits to speak, just like people leave a crowded church more slowly. Now the sanctuary of the mind is full, and thoughts bump up against other thoughts. Ideas must respect other ideas. They are not the only voice in the choir.

Most are, in fact, the children of older and wiser thoughts that came before them. A truly educated person will even hold the door for someone else's point of view."

I have never forgotten that wonderful lesson. And now, whenever I drive down the street, I see the consequences of unexamined thinking everywhere—false dichotomies springing up like weeds in the vacant lot that is America's religious and political landscape. We trade bumper sticker jabs and chew mindlessly on the cud of an either-or world.

The omnipresent yellow ribbon that says SUPPORT OUR TROOPS really carries an unstated but implicit coda: BY SUPPORTING THE WAR. But what if you support the troops but oppose the war? What if, if fact, you think the best way to support the troops is to oppose the war?

That will undermine their mission, critics say. It will send the wrong message and embolden the enemy. If this is the case, then logically speaking, war has become a form of mind control, censoring the possibility of independent thought more powerfully, as George Orwell understood, than any other tool of propaganda. Once a war begins, no matter how misbegotten, can it never be questioned?

Minds are much easier to control if they have only an on-off switch—for or against. Authoritarian leaders have always known that people are easier to control if their minds jerk as easily as their knees. Keep it simple, and you will encourage simplemindedness. Tell the world that "you're either with us or with the terrorists," and you have set the stage for the end of the world.

There is a reason why religious fundamentalists like to frame every human dilemma as a cosmic battle between good and evil. It's easy. It's comforting. And it's a powerful way to recruit warriors for the right side (which is "our" side, of course). That's why the Christian Right casts every important social issue in the rhetoric of war. There is an "enemy" out there (abortion doctors, activist judges, feminists, evolutionists, gays, New Age heretics), and they are coming to get you. They are in your schools, in your churches, in your neighborhoods. If you don't defeat them, you will be defeated by them. Satan takes no prisoners.

Oddly enough, this sounds exactly like the approach to religion that Jesus gave his life to change. Instead of drawing lines in the sand, he made a different kind of mark—drawing circles around more and more people who found themselves on the wrong side of the legal codes and ritual demarcations of the day. Instead of understanding God as demanding holiness by demanding purity (achieved by avoiding all thing unclean), Jesus insisted that God was pure Compassion and invited his followers to *imitatio dei*—an imitation of God.[1]

Instead of carefully adhering to social boundaries and avoiding contact with "untouchables," the disciples were urged to use unconditional love to break down the barriers of human contrivance. Maddening as it might seem (and obviously dangerous), the message is that the love of God is in fact universal and indiscriminate. And yet nothing, absolutely nothing, is as *disorienting* as the idea that God really does love everybody.

It's enough to make you want to take over God's job, to bring some moral order out of this suspiciously liberal divine chaos— which is precisely what many God-fearing churches have done. After all, if there are no personal advantages to being religious, nothing that will constitute a tangible return on my investment, what I am doing sitting in this pew?

The simple but almost forgotten commandment "You shall love your neighbor as yourself" is radical precisely because it presumes that we love ourselves quite a bit. And nothing drives a true believer crazy like the idea that God does indeed love infidels, idiots, and heathens just as much as he loves devout Republicans.

Luke puts this in a particularly disturbing way, especially if you are an investment banker: "If you lend to those from whom you hope to receive, what credit is that to you? Even sinners lend to sinners, to receive as much again. But love your enemies, do good, and lend, expecting nothing in return. Your reward will be great, and you will be children of the Most High; for he is kind to the ungrateful and the wicked" (Luke 6:34–35).

God is kind to the ungrateful and the wicked? Well, hallelujah!

If this is true, and we don't get to make up the Gospel as we go along, then the world has now been turned upside down. If pushing back the separations that divide the human family was the work of Jesus—until every last solitary soul is considered precious and redeemable—then the rhetoric of the Christian Right has become itself heretical. It demonizes the other instead of humanizing the other and thus carries us, and the nation, further and further away from the mind of Christ. What Bible are these guys reading?

The truth is, a remarkable number of them are not reading at all. They are watching television, and they believe what they hear. Author Bill McKibben wrote a brilliant essay in *Harper's* in which he explains the total disconnect between popular Christianity and the actual teachings of Jesus. It is rooted in a dangerous oblivion:

> Only 40 percent of Americans can name more than four of the Ten Commandments, and a scant half can cite any of the four authors of the Gospels. Twelve percent believe Joan of Arc was Noah's wife. This failure to recall the specifics of our Christian heritage may be further evidence of our nation's educational decline, but it probably doesn't matter all that much in spiritual or political terms. Here is a statistic that does matter: Three quarters of American believe the Bible teaches that "God helps those who help themselves." That is,

three out of four Americans believe that this über-American idea, a notion at the core of our current individualistic politics and culture, which was in fact uttered by Ben Franklin, actually appears in Holy Scripture. The thing is, not only is Franklin's wisdom not biblical; it's counter-biblical. Few ideas could be further from the Gospel message, with its radical summons to love of neighbor. On this essential matter, most Americans—most American *Christians*—are simply wrong, as if 75 percent of American scientists believed that Newton proved gravity causes apples to fly up.[2]

Granted, thinking is hard work, and thinking about moral and ethical issues is particularly hard work. Although the phrase "situation ethics" rolls off the tongue of the Christian Right with disdain, the fact is that there is no other kind. Jesus proved this when he forgave the woman caught in adultery.

Even so, I can appreciate the universal human desire to be certain about some things in an uncertain world. Certainty is almost intoxicating, especially when combined with the company of others who are certain about their certainty and yours. But the Christian Right takes this to mean certainty about one's position on hot-button social issues or about doctrines concerning the nature of Jesus that arose three centuries after his death.

Followers of Jesus are asked to do something much more difficult: to be certain that if their answer to a moral or ethical question is not *loving*, then it is not Christian. Either-or thinking is the antithesis of this "other-oriented" agape. By nature, it does not expand the circle of God's love like those outward-bound ripples from a stone in the proverbial pond. Dogmatic thinking regards its rigidity as a virtue and holds more flexible approaches to the spiritual life to be a sign of weakness.

Yet Christianity began as a *way of life*, not a set of creeds and doctrines demanding total agreement. In fact, it was in reaction to religion too narrowly defined by law, by ritual, and by an angry God that The Way swept through the Mediterranean world like a "mighty wind" of radical freedom. Its critics, not surprisingly, called it "soft" on just about everything.

Ironically, now that believing the right things *about* Jesus has become more important than the life to which Jesus calls us, it is Jesus himself who has become dispensable. The things that the pre-Easter Jesus taught us about God have become less important than the things the post-Easter church insists that we believe about the post-Easter Jesus.[3] The first followers of Jesus believed in radical inclusion as the essence of faith in action. They believed that it either is or is not in God's nature to want to save us all. And yet in the name of Jesus, the religious system inspired by such radical inclusion has now become a closed system and thus, paradoxically, *irreligious*.

Here is the simple but disturbing truth: at the university, it is the religion majors in my class who are invariably the most closed-minded. They seem to have partitioned their brains into two categories with a curtain of steel in between. On one side are the subjects that permit logical scrutiny, and on the other are those that don't. The subjects that must be protected from critical examination, of course, are religious doctrines, followed closely by political affinities. That's why it should come as no surprise to anyone that it is nearly impossible to reason with a fundamentalist about matters religious *or* political. Such matters are "off-limits," stored in a part of the brain labeled "inaccessible" and "inviolate." You cannot "access that file."

How odd when you consider that into his own world of religious certainty, unchallenged tradition, and spiritual bipolarity came Jesus of Nazareth to challenge the false dichotomies of his time. Again and again, in the Sermon on the Mount, he began by saying, "You have *heard* it said" (that was the old way), "but *I* say . . ." (this is the new way). In other words, what you *thought* God wanted is not what God really wants, and the standard by which *you* measure righteousness has been replaced by the reality of a new consciousness, the Kingdom of Heaven.

He spoke about it in the present tense—it is "at hand"—and in the future tense—it is "yet to come." It is me, and yet it is not only me—rather it is all of you who do the will of my Father. The Kingdom is in this moment, and yet it is not to be confused with this moment or confined to it. It goes forward in each of my disciples and in their heirs who feed the hungry, clothe the naked, and visit the sick and imprisoned.

In the meantime, troubling as it may seem, God loves Gentiles too; he loves lepers, widows, half-breeds from the hill country, the mentally ill, the blind, the forgotten, and the dispossessed. Either-or thinking is not only wrong but also dangerous to your spiritual health. God is not a lawgiver and judge. God is pure compassion.[4]

When George W. Bush decided to launch an invasion against the sovereign nation of Iraq, he had great difficulty persuading other nations to participate. He did not view this as a problem with his policy but as a problem with the thinking and resolve of those other nations. In his mind, as uncluttered as that nearly empty church, *they* "just don't get it." Far from "holding the door for someone else's idea," Bush thinks along the lines of that bumper sticker used to advertise trucks: LEAD, FOLLOW, OR BECOME ROAD KILL.

It has long been believed that humility is a sign of genuine faith. What, then, are we to make of a professing Christian who is impatient and petulant? Which part of the Sermon on the Mount counsels that our enemies be taunted? Which text recommends that those with whom we disagree are to be chided? Bush's response to all those who refused to join the "coalition of the willing" was to imply that they are "unwilling" and thus foolish. The idea that *he* might be wrong and almost everybody else might be right simply never entered his mind.

Now, in the spirit of the cleansing of the Temple, we are going to have to start turning over the tables of apathy and complicity in our own time. If the purpose of the Judeo-Christian prophetic tradition is to speak truth to power, then the time has come to stand up and do just that.

This war is not, nor has it ever been, about "us versus them." It is not about freedom versus tyranny or democracy versus tribal fanaticism. It has been, from the beginning, about us and our economic needs. It *is* about oil and always has been. The real purpose of this war, hatched in the minds of those who believed we would be greeted as liberators and given flowers,[5] came long before 9/11 and the coveted Pearl Harbor moment.

It was not to protect us against nonexistent threats from nonexistent weapons of mass destruction or to spread American-style democracy (with all its faults) to the rest of the world. The honest-to-God reason for this war was and remains to establish permanent military bases in the Middle East and to protect access to and control over the precious oil reserves to which we are precariously addicted.

All other rationales now have that hollow ring that accompanies the apologetics of men too ashamed of their real motives to tell us the truth. They seduce us with flags, soldier worship, and marshal music—like a man who writes poetry to the woman he is trying to bed. He shines his shoes, combs his hair, and tells her at length that what he really cares about is *her* future, *her* children, *her* dignity. Time is of the essence, of course, because other suitors are lining up outside her door, dreaming of their own key to her energy-rich bedroom. "The greatest single prize in all history," as Daniel Yergin calls it in his Pulitzer Prize–winning book, is as base as it is unbearable: "It's the oil, stupid."[6]

Chapter Five

The National Debt, Family Values, and Why They Hate Us

> When you fail to veto a single spending bill but ask us to pay for a war with no exit strategy and no end in sight, creating an enormous deficit that hangs like a great millstone around the necks of our children, you are doing something immoral.

The triumph of today's Republican Party can be summed up in one phrase: *family values*. Every conservative politician alive today has learned to harness the power of these two magic words, even though the nuclear family to which it alludes is increasingly rare. Using what George Lakoff, a linguistics professor, calls the "strict father morality" model to define the heart of the conservative conceptual system,[1] the Republicans have joined forces with the Christian Right to persuade millions of middle-class families to vote against their own economic self-interest in order to "save" the family from extinction and the nation from moral collapse.

Believing that laissez-faire capitalism is not only the best economic system but the most moral as well, the Christian Right has reversed the church's long-standing notion that unchecked private ambition is a form of greed. Now it is a form of "works righteousness," and riches are a sign of God's favor. Free enterprise works because it is moral; it is moral because it works.

When such a religious endorsement is extended into the political arena, a strict father morality becomes a strict father economic policy. Republicans are therefore cutting taxes not because they wish to enrich themselves, they tell us, but because "Father knows best" what to do with his own money. Ours is the party of self-discipline, individual responsibility, and tough love, they say. Theirs (the Democrats) is the party of self-indulgence, a victim mentality, and free love.

The commander in chief of the strict father family values movement is James Dobson, founder of the most powerful Christian Right political lobbying empire in America, Focus on the Family. He is not a minister or a politician but a psychologist whose views on parenting in the 1960s stood in stark contrast to the essence of what Lakoff regards as the liberal conceptual system: the "nurturant parent morality."[2]

Just how do you recognize a "strict" father? According to Lakoff, he sees the world as dangerous, with evil lurking everywhere, especially in the human soul. He is the unquestioned authority figure in the family and teaches the children right from wrong, enforcing the rules through rewards and punishments. He shows love and appreciation when his children follow the rules but never coddles them, lest they become spoiled. Dobson summed it all up nicely once when he explained how to handle a rebellious child. In his early book, *Dare to Discipline*, he wrote, "When a youngster tries this kind of stiff-necked rebellion, you had better take it out of him, and pain is a marvelous purifier."[3]

The worldview that underlies the strict father morality is based on what Lakoff calls "folk behaviorism." In short, "people, left to their own devices, tend simply to satisfy their desires. But people will make themselves do things they don't want to do in order to get rewards; they will refrain from doing things they do want to do in order to avoid punishment."[4]

This rather dismal view of human nature, that without rewards people will not do the right thing and that without fear of punishment they will do the wrong things, stands in stark contrast to the biblical view that humans are created in the image of God, "a little lower than the angels"—what the letter to the Ephesians calls "God's masterpiece."

What's more, the image of God as a Strict Father, which permeates orthodox Christianity, has been politicized by the Christian Right. God is the Father who knows best and operates the universe on a system of sensible, even predictable, rewards and punishments. In a world of rapid change and complicated new family relationships, this is enormously comforting and nostalgic, in much the same way that old black-and-white TV sitcoms feel warm and fuzzy.

The only problem with the Strict Father view of God is that it stands in stark contrast to the most familiar and beloved father-son parable told by Jesus. If ever a son was disobedient, disrespectful, and self-indulgent, it was the Prodigal Son (Luke 15:11–32). If ever a father needed to be strict and not coddle, it was the father of the Prodigal Son.

He takes his share of his inheritance early; blows it on wine, women, and song; and ends up disgracing the family name by working in a pigsty—a Jew feeding an unclean animal. When he comes to his senses (runs out of money) and decides to go home and apologize to his father, the old man sees him coming home across the field and does not play the role of strict father at all. There is no lecture, no tough love, not even a well-deserved "Do you know how disappointed your mother and I feel?"

Instead of peering over his paper in silence or asking, "Did you learn your lesson?" this elderly man *runs* to meet his youngest son and embraces him with joy and thanksgiving. He orders up a party, kills the fatted calf, and has his servants bring a robe and a ring for the royal reunion. Why? Because, in the words of a loving father, "My son was dead and is alive, was lost and is found."

The elder son, meanwhile, who played by the rules and never shamed his father, is furious. He never got a party like this, and so he stands outside the house fuming with resentment. His father tries to explain his joy at receiving his younger brother home safe and reassures him, saying, "Son, you are always with me, and all that is mine is yours." It falls on deaf ears. The elder son's most basic understanding of fairness, enforced by appropriate rewards and punishments, has been violated. The only song he feels like singing is "O How I Hate Amazing Grace!"

If this parable is a metaphor for God, and God's extravagant welcome, then we've got a big problem with strict father morality and its political manifestations. The God of the Christian Right says, "Watch out!" while the God of Jesus says, "Welcome home!" Ernest Campbell summed up the American church this way: "We've got a Loving Father Gospel in an Elder Brother Church."[5] Spare the rod and spoil the child? Apparently that's not what Jesus believed. It was more like "Spare the love and lose the child."

All of this has political implications, of course, as "Father knows best" theology is co-opted by "Father knows best" politicians. One might conclude, therefore, that we are now living in the time of a strict father government. Or are we? One of the things we all used to take for granted was that conservatives were *fiscally* conservative, in that pay-as-you-go Goldwater sort of way. Democrats were the party of big government and big spending, goes the familiar refrain, but Republicans are cautious and frugal and believe in balanced budgets and in "helping those who helped themselves." Not anymore.

Republicans now practice what they have never preached—expanding the federal government by record spending and record deficits. From Reagan forward, Republicans have been the big spenders. A combination of tax cuts for the wealthy and huge increases in military spending have us all drowning in a sea of red ink. When the national bill comes due, it can only be paid in pain. But it will be paid by *others*, especially by our children.

Father knows best? He knows what is best for himself and his peers in the corporate world. As for the children, the ones from whom we have all borrowed the future, if they are watching carefully, they will learn how to borrow against the future of their children some day. Believe me, the children are watching.

So much for Luke's counsel: "If you have not been trustworthy in handling worldly wealth, who will trust you with true riches?

And if you have not been trustworthy with someone else's property, who will give you property of your own?" (Luke 16:11–12 NIV). As it turns out, financial self-discipline is what many conservatives insist that *others* practice. Tough love is what God favors for the poor. Welfare is what single mothers receive, not what corporations gobble up. Generosity toward oneself and stinginess toward others may be the credo of our time, but it reverses the counsel of every faith tradition in the world. In fact, it might be more accurate to say that instead of living in the age of strict father government, we are actually living in the time of the self-indulgent father.

In this model, the father is entitled to enrich himself by taking risks with other people's money, but the children must still be taught to do without so that they will not be spoiled. The real ethic here is to get all you can, while you can, and let others be grateful for the crumbs that fall from the table.

As of this writing, President Bush has yet to veto a single spending bill brought to him by the Republican-controlled House and Senate. The party that professes to hate waste, graft, and corruption has now raised the bar for all three. The political conservatives who once favored not spending more money than we collect have now taken the surplus they inherited from the Clinton administration and in record time turned it into the most ominous, monumental debt in U.S. history.[6]

What's more, by the simple yet immoral act of not including the cost of the war in Iraq in the deficit, this administration encourages an already oblivious culture to avoid facing reality. The truth is that the national debt is one of the gravest but most underreported stories of our time. The media find it boring when compared to Hollywood scandals or the latest diet fad. Besides, who can even *fathom* such a sum of money?

On a recent trip to New York City, my wife and I stood for a few minutes under the most frightening marquee in the nation: the national debt clock, a "scoreboard" of sorts, ticking off the trillions we have borrowed from our kids. Under the $7 trillion figure that grows by thousands every second, the bottom figure showed "your family's share"—now approaching $100,000. It's enough to make you wonder: if this is what people do who grew up singing "Jesus Loves the Little Children," exactly what might we expect from heathens?

In the church, we like to talk about the importance of "mindfulness." It is a virtue to be aware of the consequences of everything we do. The abandonment of old-fashioned "conservative" principles in the runaway deficit is therefore the height of *mindlessness*. It is not unlike people who don't know, and don't seem to care, how much interest they are paying on their credit cards. They are seduced by schemes that promise instant gratification but delayed payments. It's all about *now*. As for the children, we really do love them. They are the future, you know?

Come to think of it, protecting *innocence* is very important to the Christian Right. The unborn child's life is innocent, so it deserves protection, while the death row inmate's life does not. But every single child in American today is entirely innocent of the financial crimes being committed against them. These children are innocent, but they will pay as if they were guilty.

One of the most powerful ideas in the American psyche is that parents want to see their children surpass them and enjoy a better life than they did. We are witnessing the *reversal* of that fond hope in our time by heaping burning coals of debt upon their heads. They will have to do without because we could not say enough is enough. Many will be denied basic necessities because we mortgaged their future to finance our conspicuous consumption. And they will pay for this hopeless war for a lifetime—if not with their lives, then with their dreams of prosperity.

What's more, our cultural love of children, those precious "angels" about which a vast sentimental industry has now sprung up, are looking good on Glamour Shots, Hallmark cards, and *American Idol*. But in real life, the picture is not so rosy. In real life, almost one in five American children lives in poverty, and when it comes to any measure of how the strong are treating the weak—childhood nutrition, infant mortality, access to preschool—we are nearly last among the rich nations.[7]

How is it that in less overtly religious nations like Sweden and Norway, the statistics are so much better? The schools there are so much brighter, the playgrounds are so much safer, and no child grows up without access to basic health insurance and lifelong health care. They have higher taxes, of course. Does that mean they are not a Christian nation?

The answer we hear from the strict father Christian Right is this: work harder, pray harder, and if you are deserving, God will bless you. Like the ancient belief that human misfortune was an inheritance—"Rabbi, who sinned, this man or his parents, that he should be born blind?" (John 9:2)—the great unspoken truth behind the Christian Right's view of poverty is that the poor *deserve* it. They are being punished by a strict Father God, and who are we to interfere with the divine system for rewarding some and punishing others?

The answer is: all of us who care about the Gospel. The ministry of Jesus was never based on what someone deserved. There is never a questionnaire given out in advance of a healing. There is no effort to determine whether human misery was caused by circumstances beyond our control or by miserable human beings. The saint heals because it is in the nature of love to heal. The politician asks, "Are you part of the 'deserving' or 'undeserving' poor?"

Marcus Borg reminds us that a strict father model for God is linguistically misleading with regard to gender. "In Hebrew (as well as in Aramaic), the word usually translated as 'compassion' is the plural of a noun that in its singular form means 'womb.' In the Hebrew Bible, *compassion* is both a feeling and a way of being that flows out of that feeling."[8]

As for the idea that material abundance is a sign of God's favor, what are we to make of the parable in Luke 12:16–21 in which a rich man tears down perfectly good barns and builds new, larger ones, only to have his soul suddenly required of him and come up empty-handed? That parable indicts the idea that abundance carries with it no responsibility to the community where most people lived on the edge of starvation. You really *can't* take it with you, but if you have it now, you are supposed to share. Perhaps the most ignored passage in the Bible is the one that never gets preached on in wealthy churches: "From everyone to whom much has been given, much will be required; and from the one to whom much has been entrusted, even more will be demanded" (Luke 12:48).

As for the coveted nuclear family, it can be a wonderful thing, but it was apparently not all that important to Jesus. Once, when his family came looking for him and he was informed that his mother and brothers were standing outside wanting to speak to him, he improvised the definition of family right on the spot. It had nothing to do with biology and everything to do with behavior. "Who is my mother, and who are my brothers? And pointing to his disciples, he said, 'Here are my mother and my brothers! For whoever does the will of my Father in heaven is my brother and sister and mother'" (Matthew 12:47–50).

One of the most familiar images of Jesus in American church life is that of the gentle shepherd sitting down with a group of children who have been brought to him for a blessing. They are scattered at his feet, looking scrubbed and radiant, as a heavenly beam of light falls on his forehead. The children are all well behaved, and not a single one is losing a diaper or screaming his or her little head off.

They all look up at him as he looks down on them—and then he pronounces a blessing on their innocence and purity, "for it is to such as these that the kingdom of heaven belongs" (Matthew 19:14). A less well known but much more ominous text, however, concerns the fate of anyone who would harm a child or make children's lives more difficult: "If any of you put a stumbling block before one of these little ones who believe in me, it would be better for you if a great millstone were fastened around your neck and you were drowned in the depths of the sea" (Matthew 18:6–7).

The national debt is just such a stumbling block. It is the antithesis of "family values." It is neither pro-life nor pro-child. It is, instead, a economic version of the plagues, sent out by a modern pharaoh upon his own house.

> When you cause most of the rest of the world to hate a country
> that was once the most loved country in the world and act as if
> it doesn't matter what others think of us, only what God thinks
> of you, you have done something immoral.

Every major poll taken in the last few years tells the same sad story: the reputation of the United States in the eyes of the rest of the world has taken a beating, especially in the years since 9/11. Although many people are quick to separate their visceral hatred of George W. Bush from their feelings about the country as a whole, the distinction is hardly comforting. Leaders, after all, do symbolize the nations they lead—especially in what is reputed to be the world's leading democracy. Did the nation's citizens not elect this man?

Stranger still is the president's apparent lack of concern for America's reputation. To the contrary, he wears his disdain for the opinion of others like a badge of honor and ridicules them for not appreciating our self-evident superiority: "They just don't get it." If Thomas Aquinas was correct when he named the deadly sin of pride as the cause of every other sin, it's no wonder that they hate us. Petulance and arrogance are one thing in a teenager; they are quite another in the leader of the world's only superpower.

Sadly, it has not always been this way. In fact, despite our obvious and even horrific mistakes, America could count itself among the most admired nations after World War II. The depth of our sacrifice in stopping both German and Japanese fascism endeared us to a grateful world. Our educational institutions were considered the best, and our edgy pop culture was both admired and imitated. We could be loud, overbearing, and outrageous, of course, but we also seemed to stand on certain principles and were prepared to make sacrifices for others.

Our Achilles' heel has always been, however, the gap between our noble rhetoric and our actual behavior. As Samuel Johnson noted long ago, many perceived us as a freedom-loving people engaged in less than admirable practices. Americans, in Johnson's eyes, were "thieves" in their relations with indigenous peoples and African slaves. "How is it that we hear the loudest yelps for liberty among the drivers of Negroes? . . . I am willing to love all mankind, except an American."[9]

For the same reason that many young people walk away from organized religion ("They talk the talk but don't walk the walk"), the international community has come to see American foreign policy in the second half of the twentieth century as rank hypocrisy. Vietnam was a disaster at home and abroad, with an estimated six hundred thousand civilians killed. Use of Agent Orange for deforestation had devastating long-term environmental effects. But perhaps no single aspect of our foreign policy has so angered the world as our long-standing practice of first supporting brutal dictators when they are useful to us and then later demonizing and destroying them when they're not.

Whether it's Noriega, Marcos, or Saddam Hussein, we proved repeatedly that our friends are our friends until we decide they are our enemies. It was the United States that supplied Saddam Hussein with poison gas, military advisers, and arms when he was fighting against Iran in the 1980s. When he used the gas and the Senate passed a bill to condemn it, President Ronald Reagan threatened to veto the bill. Saddam was our "friend" and got a warm handshake in 1983 from Donald Rumsfeld. Later the same voices would call him the "Butcher of Baghdad."[10]

Our support of the Afghan mujahedin against the Soviet occupation may have sowed the seeds of 9/11. After arming them, we later had to fight them. Then we allied ourselves with their Northern Alliance because they were fighting the Taliban. By then, the country we had used as a borrowed battlefield (like so many others) was awash in weapons and serving as a training ground for terrorists. Our policies in Central America were similar and equally disastrous.

Although we like to think of ourselves as the most "civilized" nation in the world, "there is a difference," the activist preacher William

Sloane Coffin Jr. pointed out, "between a great nation and just a very large country." We continue to practice capital punishment, even though most of the rest of the civilized world considers it barbaric. When the International Criminal Court was established in 2002 as a permanent tribunal for crimes against humanity and genocide, the Bush administration withdrew support in order to shield our soldiers and policies from its jurisdiction. Every democratic nation on earth has signed on to ICC except the United States and Israel, the latter fearing that its policies toward the Palestinians would subject it to ICC proceedings.

We are both the most overtly "religious" nation on earth, and yet the most violent, with the highest rate of gun ownership in the world. We also incarcerate a larger percentage of our population than any nation on earth—mostly nonviolent drug offenders who become "clients" in private prisons. We also produce the most violent movies and video games on the planet and export them to that vast coalition of the "unwilling." American law enforcement conducts a "war on drugs" at the supply end, while American citizens buy more illegal drugs than anyone, keeping in business the very drug lords we are sworn to defeat.

We use soaring rhetoric about freedom and equality and yet the ratio of women to men in positions of power is still shameful. Only four other First World nations—Japan, Hungary, Italy, and Ireland— have a smaller percentage of women in politics than the United States. We defend free speech for ourselves but deny it to others. We preach free trade unless our companies can't compete, in which case we demand tariffs. We have the "right" to possess nuclear weapons, of course, but certain other countries do not—even though we are the only country ever to drop a nuclear weapon on a civilian population.

We do all this while lecturing the rest of the world on morality and labeling other countries as "evil." We pray for our soldiers and their families at the National Day of Prayer, put IN GOD WE TRUST on our money, and insist that schoolchildren proclaim allegiance to "one Nation, under God" in the Pledge of Allegiance—yet we claim to be a nation founded on the separation of church and state.

The "English only" movement and the monolinguistic arrogance of many Americans living abroad is seen as a double standard, and the growing Americanization of the world through our fast-food and entertainment exports is often resented by other countries. We have a way of thinking we know what is best for everyone, and yet we would never accept such control over our own social and sexual mores. Wal-Mart and McDonald's are now such powerful corporate entities that they can set up shop anywhere and stamp out the local competition—and with it the local culture and economy. The net effect is that more people than ever perceive Americans as both arrogant and greedy—two vices that represent the antithesis of the Gospel that 85 percent of us claim to follow.

Our obsession with "being number one," our idolatry of the American flag, and our jingoistic claim that we are "the greatest nation that has ever existed on the face of the earth" strikes more and more non-Americans as both offensive and out of touch with reality. Because we haven't seen an international war on our own soil since 1812 and have never been invaded, many people, especially Europeans, think that Americans have lost all comprehension of the horrors of war. Media coverage of warfare is so one-sided that it has become a form of corporate propaganda.[11]

But when it comes to raising the ire of the world, perhaps nothing compares with our insatiable appetite for material possessions and our wanton disregard for the environment. We outconsume and outpollute everyone in the world, and yet we did not ratify the Kyoto Protocol because it would exempt developing nations and hurt U.S. businesses. Instead of leading the world toward conservation, alternative fuels, and sustainable agricultural and business practices, we are dragging our feet out of self-interest and giving religion a very bad name in the process.

At its core, the life of faith is about *selflessness*, not selfishness. If we live by grace, which is a central tenet of the Gospel, then we know that Creation itself, and every breath we take, is a gift. We did not make ourselves or this garden of a planet that sustains us. What, then, does it mean to be "pro-life" beyond a particular position in the abortion debate? The most profoundly pro-life people I've ever met have been simple-living, peace-loving people like the Quakers and Mennonites, who live to protect *everything,* not just the unborn.

They possess what the great rabbi Abraham Heschel calls "radical amazement,"[12] and it makes them humble, grateful, and self-possessed. If these are the essential dispositions of a person of faith, then their opposites must be the essence of the irreligious: arrogance, ingratitude, and insecurity. Unfortunately, this is the image that much of the world now sees in our so-called Christian nation. The reason they hate us is painfully simple. We have become the hypocrites that Jesus rebuked: "Woe to you scribes and Pharisees, hypocrites! For you tithe mint, dill, and cumin and have neglected the weightier matters of the law: justice and mercy and faith. It is these you ought to have practiced without neglecting the others. You blind guides! You strain out a gnat but swallow a camel!" (Matthew 23:23–24).

Chapter Six

Homosexuals and
the Politics of Death

When you use hatred of homosexuals as a wedge issue to turn
out record numbers of evangelical voters and seek to use the
Constitution as a tool of discrimination, you are doing something immoral.

So it has come down to this. The Christian Right, speaking as if with
God's own voice, has drawn a bright line in the ecclesiastical sand:
homosexuality is a sin, they tell us, "incompatible with Christian
teaching." Our gay sons and daughters, members of our own families,
who are a "fact of Creation" and a timeless constituency of God's
world, are said to be sinful in eyes of the Creator who made them?
They cannot be ordained to the ministry, we are told, or allowed to
marry. They must be "cured" and their "lifestyle" must be condemned.

When the history of our age is written, I believe with all my
heart that this will be seen as yet one more of the church's colossal
mistakes—along with the embrace of slavery, the subordination of
women, and institutional racism. This plague on the body of Christ,
and the vitriolic rhetoric that surrounds it, will be remembered as a
source of deep shame. It has eaten away at the soul of the church,
dividing congregations, denominations, families, and the nation. It
has become the mother of all political wedge issues—the bottom
line for Karl Rove's strategy of divide and conquer.

The issue for many of us in the church is not what "causes" homosexuality (we don't know) or whether acceptance of our gay brothers and sisters is an endorsement of sexual promiscuity (of course it isn't) but whether the Church of Jesus Christ is going to be true to its own founding principle: *radical hospitality*. The Gospel specializes in human beings who are left out but deserve to be invited in. Either we believe it when we say that God loves everybody, or we don't.

And please don't give me that tired line: "Love the sinner, hate the sin." We need to have a thoughtful, prayerful, gracious conversation in the church about sexual orientation, not just about sexual behavior. We're talking here about what someone *is*, not what someone *does*. The handful of condemnations against homosexuality in the Bible are directed at homosexual activities, which were considered unnatural because they were nonprocreative and idolatrous because they were grouped with activities that were believed to separate us from God. They were not directed against sexual orientation, which nobody understood in those days and which we still don't understand today.

The importance of this distinction is revealed when the Christian Right makes what it believes to be a charitable compromise: asking homosexuals to be celibate. The unspoken premise here is that we can forgive a condition that we consider to be an aberration, but we cannot countenance a behavior that we consider to be repulsive. It is the church's own version of "don't ask, don't tell."

Yet what the church is called to do is to encourage human beings to practice integrity, honesty, and self-discipline—whether gay or straight. We could make a quantum leap forward in the church's struggle with this issue if we could just make it clear that inclusiveness and sexual integrity are not mutually exclusive. Acceptance of gays in the church is not an endorsement of a "lifestyle," when that word is used as a euphemism for flamboyant promiscuity, but a response to the call of Jesus to welcome every human being into the full sacramental hospitality of the Kingdom. This is not a compromise of "standards" but is in fact a willingness to extend them to more and more human beings.

Having said this, and knowing that most of my evangelical sisters and brothers do not agree, I am less dismayed by honest disagreement than by the appropriation of the issue as a political tool. If the final act of grace is to make a person gracious, then the final perversion of Christianity is to use fear and loathing as an instrument of power. When an issue this complicated and divisive splits the body politic, a gracious leader will always seek dialogue and compromise. He will never exploit the controversy for political gain.

That is, of course, unless his political adviser wants to turn out four million evangelical voters in a close national election using the gay marriage issue to "energize the base." Karl Rove did exactly that, and eleven battleground states drafted anti–gay marriage amendments to coincide with the election. They all passed overwhelmingly and brought out a record numbers of what pollsters say was the decisive "moral" vote.[1]

At the same time, the president was calling for an amendment to the U.S. Constitution banning same-sex marriage for exactly the same purpose. He knew it would never pass, but in order to choreograph the appearance of indignation, he followed the script. Since the election, we haven't heard another word from the president about a gay marriage amendment. That is, until the midterm elections that are now upon us.

It is difficult to know which is worse: co-opting antigay sentiment in the church for political gain or attempting to use the Constitution as a tool of discrimination. Consider this: just over four decades ago, a southern preacher named Martin Luther King Jr. used that same Constitution as a national "text" for one of the most memorable sermons in American history. Reminding us of the expansive promises of our founding document, King compared what we say we believe to what we actually practice and challenged us to live up to our own "scripture." "We hold these truths to be self-evident, that all men are created equal." And then he added, "Yes, black men as well as white men."[2]

Now, within the span of a single generation, we have a president who attempts to use the same founding document in a restrictive way, enshrining a particular religious belief into a constitution born to disentangle church and state and serve the people as a shield, not as a sword. In the end, it is difficult to decide whether the tactics are most frightening or the lack of outrage from "the people" to whom the Constitution belongs.

In his book *The Sins of Scripture*, Episcopal Bishop John Shelby Spong describes this battle over homosexuality as having "all the intensity of the final battle of Armageddon that is supposed to mark the end of the world. . . . The stakes are thought to be so high that many people on both sides assert that Christianity itself will die if the other side prevails."[3]

The issue of acceptance (which one side considers to be the collapse of Christian morality itself) or nonacceptance (which the other side considers to be the end of the church as a meaningful institution) has caused completely new configurations to emerge in Christendom. The Vatican actively courts other communions, otherwise considered to be "outside the truth," so long as they will join forces in condemning homosexuality as unnatural and deviant. Meanwhile, as Bishop Spong points out, Rome knows "full well that its ordained ranks are liberally populated with gay persons." Furthermore, the requirement that priests be celibate "has provided a safe haven in which gay men could escape the social pressure of marrying while being able to suggest by implication that they are motivated only by virtue and the sacrifice of answering a 'higher calling.'"[4]

What is at stake here, of course, is the authority of Scripture itself, which seems to be unraveling not just among "secular humanists" but among confessing Christians as well. Yet there have long been faithful Christians who do not take every word of the Bible literally. What's more, they consider that to do so would destroy their faith. It was Augustine who said that "when I understood literally, I was slain spiritually."[5]

The most familiar texts cited to prove that "God hates homosexuality" are Leviticus 18:22, "You shall not lie with a male as with a woman; it is an abomination," and Leviticus 20:13, "If a man lies with a male as with a woman, both of them have committed an

abomination; they shall be put to death; their blood be upon them."
These admonitions were written in the sixth century B.C.E. by Jewish religious leaders who were trying to help save the existence of a captive people by the institution of what is known as the "holiness code." Whether it was the establishment of the Sabbath, kosher dietary laws, or circumcision, the holiness code helped keep the exiled Jews separate from their captors—and that included a clear delineation from their captors' sexual practices as well.

Other commandments from the holiness code are either unknown or ignored, and they include a host of primitive practices that may strike us today as either amusing or barbaric. "You shall not round off the hair on your temples or mar the edges of your beard" (Leviticus 19:27) is God's law for barbers, but "a man or woman who is a medium or spiritualist among you must be put to death. You are to stone them" (Leviticus 20:27) is no laughing matter. Out of this ancient code, however, we lift two texts condemning homosexuality and prescribing death as punishment for it. These are singled out as the "inviolate Word of God" because they appear to give biblical credence to our own prejudice and fear.

There is a growing body of scientific evidence to suggest that homosexuality is not a moral choice but a biological predisposition, much like being born left-handed (also the source of fear and condemnation in the Bible) or with red hair. But until the issue has been definitively answered, the church has a sacred responsibility with regard to what happens in the meantime, what the poet W. H. Auden called "the time being." It is, he said, "the most trying time of all."[6]

Love is our credo. Reconciliation is our assignment. Abundant life is our quest. Therefore, we must not be defined by our disagreements. People of goodwill can disagree, but homophobia and Christianity are incompatible.

In the 1980s, when the AIDS epidemic first appeared, President Reagan refused for years to acknowledge it or even to mention the disease publicly.[7] A crusader for "moral values," Reagan did what many people do when faced with unpleasant realities: he ignored them. That silence cost lives, and the rancor in the church today over homosexuality is doing the same thing. It is killing people.

The suicide rate among gay teens is alarming, and the risky sexual behavior that the Christian Right condemns is actually encouraged by lack of dialogue, broken family relationships, and a culture of denial. As such, it is the antithesis of "pro-life." There is hardly a parish minister in the land who can't tell the story of some young man who realizes he is gay, only to keep the secret from his family out of fear that they will cast him out. Many of the teen runaways walking the streets of major cities are gay and lesbian and have been banished from "Christian" homes.

All of this raises a deeper issue that the church can no longer avoid. Religious fanaticism itself is a symptom of compensatory behavior. The most rigid, the most compulsive, the most paranoid religious devotees are often hiding their own dark secrets. They seek the rigidity of authoritarian systems in order to cope with their own feelings of shame. Their inner conflicts are turned outward, and the collateral damage is all too apparent.

When Jimmy Swaggart was at the peak of his evangelistic powers, preaching most powerfully against the "depravities of the flesh" and condemning the adultery of Jim Bakker and Marvin Gorman, he was also a regular customer of prostitutes in New Orleans. When photographs proved that he was a red-light regular, he tearfully resigned his ministry in 1987 but is now back on television and preaching to millions.[8] Was his preaching an attempt at self-persuasion?

In my own ministry, I have noticed an unmistakable pattern, and it is more than mere coincidence. The most homophobic people I've ever met do not live comfortably inside their own sexual skin. One friend of mine swore he would never enter a restaurant if he knew there was a gay man working inside (looking back on it, I'm surprised he ever went out to eat!). He also bought his teenage son a subscription to *Playboy* in order to help "guarantee" that his son would be a healthy, horny heterosexual. This is how little we really know about human sexuality.

When this ignorance is combined with equally uninformed "proof-texting" (selecting certain passages to prove your point while ignoring others), the results can be deadly. The story of Sodom and Gomorrah is used to justify hostility toward homosexuals, even though the real sin of the city is inhospitality, and the God it reveals is so primitive, and the view of women so base, that it should never be quoted to defend anything. When the words of Paul are quoted, especially Romans 1, there is far more to the story than meets the eye. Homosexuality is here defined as a *punishment* by God for failure to worship God properly. As a devoted rabbinical student, Paul knew that the Torah prescribed death for those who did not repress their homosexuality. And yet Paul makes repeated references to his own struggle with a "thorn in the flesh," which "dwells in my members" and leads him to proclaim that "nothing good dwells within me, that is my flesh. . . . Oh wretched man that I am, who will deliver me from this body of death?" (Romans 7:24).

What sort of agony is this? What distant memory is tormenting his flesh? When he oscillates back and forth in his writing between praise and shame, his final verdict is that nothing will be able to separate us from the love of God in Christ Jesus our Lord (Romans 8:39). And in the list of things that might do so (hardship, distress, persecution, famine, peril, or sword), he adds the revealing word *nakedness*. Bishop Spong, among others, has concluded that "Paul of Tarsus was a gay man, deeply repressed, self-loathing, rigid in denial . . . , condemning other gay people so that he can keep his own homosexuality inside the rigid discipline of his faith."[9]

If this is true, the irony runs even deeper: the words of a first-century latent homosexual, who found salvation in the saving grace of God through Jesus Christ, are now used to condemn and persecute twenty-first-century homosexuals. If it is not true, but the source of Paul's anguish involved some other "thorn" of the flesh, then it remains a matter of psychosexual repression. We fear in others what we do not have under our own control. We go through the world shadow-boxing with our own demons. Or as my friend Rabbi David Packman put it, "A man who does not love himself wisely and well will make a casualty out of the neighbor sooner or later."

The simple, undeniable truth is that the Christian Right has employed a strategy of vilification of gays for political gain, and the president has been a willing pawn. Even though the majority of Americans favor equal rights for gays, the far-right wing of the Republican party feeds on antigay rhetoric while wrapping the entire package in Christian piety. Mississippi Senator Trent Lott once equated gays with alcoholics and kleptomaniacs,[10] and it has long been a central tenet of the Christian Right that gays are "diseased" and can be "cured" using "reparative therapy." It does not seem to matter that there is no credible evidence to support the success of such therapy, which usually involves having gay men play football and repair cars while lesbians wear dresses and put on makeup.

Preachers have called AIDS a "punishment by God" and have referred to gays as having a "death-style." Research studies about gay teens and average life expectancy for gay men are notoriously misrepresented or completely fabricated to suit political ideology. The discredited research done by Paul Cameron in the early 1980s (conducted by studying obituaries in prominent gay papers in major American urban centers) concluded that life expectancy for gay males is around forty years old. The same study, using small and unrepresentative samples, concluded that you are fifteen times more likely to be killed by a homosexual than by a heterosexual during a sexual murder spree, that homosexuals have committed the most sexual conspiracy murders, and that half of those who murder out of a sexual rage are homosexuals. He also "concluded" that less than 2 percent of gay men survive to old age and that lesbians have a median age of death of forty-five. Who is Paul Cameron? He is not a scientist but the chairman of the Family Research Institute, a right-wing think tank in Washington.[11]

Rumors are constantly circulating that gays are pedophiles when in fact pedophilia is almost exclusively a heterosexual crime. Likewise, the mantra of "special rights" for homosexuals is heard in almost every political debate, even though antidiscrimination legislation grants no special rights. The Reverend Pat Robertson, who gave new meaning to the term "pro-life" by calling for the assassination of the president of Venezuela, once told his TV viewers, "I just don't think we should craft laws that give privileges on the basis of the way people perform sex acts."[12] In fact, current laws do just that—for straights.

When the Reverend Don Wildmon of the American Family Association wrote to raise funds for his organization, he used the following appeal: "For the sake of our children and society, we must OPPOSE the spread of homosexual activity! Just as we must oppose murder, stealing, and adultery! Since homosexuals cannot reproduce, the only way for them to 'breed' is to RECRUIT! And who are their targets for recruitment? Children!"[13]

These are the words of ordained Christian ministers. But they should not be not the last word. Clergy from all traditions, and from divergent theological positions, need to enter the temple of this nonsense and begin driving out the Gospel-changers with a whip. Our tepid response to the rise of the Christian Right has only encouraged a vast cross section of bright, idealistic Americans to give up on the church. Who can blame them?

When my own congregation in Oklahoma voted to become "Open and Affirming," there was not a single dissenting vote cast. Although we are a predominantly straight church, gay and lesbian persons have been part of our congregation for years—teaching Sunday school, serving on boards and committees, and adding immeasurably to our common life. After the vote was made public, a wary fellow minister saw me at the grocery store and asked, "So . . . what happened?"

I wasn't sure that I understood the question. "What do you mean 'What happened?'"

"What happened when you became a gay church?" he continued.

"We're not a gay church," I replied. "We are a Christian church."

He paused and said, "Don't you worry about your Sunday school kids?"

When my own national denomination, the United Church of Christ, tried to air a series of television commercials that demonstrate the UCC's commitment to the "extravagant welcome" of Jesus, the ads were refused by CBS and NBC because they were deemed "too controversial." One ad showed two "bouncers" in front of a church allowing some patrons to enter (white, affluent heterosexuals), while denying entry to others (a Hispanic man, a little girl of color, a person in a wheelchair, and an obviously gay couple). Then a screen message followed: JESUS DIDN'T TURN ANYONE AWAY. NEITHER DO WE.

Then came a voice-over that hardly seems "controversial": "The United Church of Christ. . . . No matter who you are, or where you are on life's journey, you're welcome here."

As the networks sought to explain their decision not to air the ads, ABC said it has a policy against "commercials with reference to religious doctrine and/or religious themes in commercial advertising." Not long after, ABC aired a commercial from Focus on the Family, claiming that it was not a religious organization.

But by far the most revealing reason came from a CBS memo produced during that network's deliberations over whether to expose the American public to an idea this radical. A group of prominent evangelical ministers had been given a special screening of the ads and were incensed at the implication that their church did not welcome gays. With the voice of the Christian Right literally breathing down their necks, one executive wrote the following: "Because this commercial touches on the exclusion of gay couples and other minority groups by other individuals and organizations, and the fact that the Executive Branch has recently proposed a Constitutional Amendment to define marriage as a union between a man and a woman, this spot is unacceptable for broadcast on the [CBS and UPN] networks."[14]

Since when do the actions of the executive branch determine which religious messages gets heard and which don't? And how is it that one church message of welcome is judged "too controversial" while countless other messages of exclusion and even hatred are standard fare? At the time of this controversy, we had just completed the nastiest, the most juvenile national campaign ever waged for the presidency. The networks had accepted ads steeped in fear, innuendo, and outright deception. Then, just a few weeks before Christmas, one church's message of hospitality in the name of Jesus was deemed unfit for broadcast in this God-fearing land. There might be children watching.[15]

Patience is indeed a virtue, but too much patience in the face of injustice becomes a sin. It would be one thing for someone like Pat Robertson to say, as he did on his *700 Club*, that homosexuals "want to come into churches and disrupt church services and throw blood all around and try to give people AIDS and spit in the face of ministers,"[16] but it is entirely another for the rest of us to keep quiet! He knows that's a lie, just like the argument that there is "clear teaching in the Bible" against homosexuality is a lie. In fact, the Christian Right seems increasingly committed to defending the indefensible, while an anxious nation watches its most public preachers self-destruct.

The French philosopher Emmanuel Levinas taught his students to understand all of human existence as the "encounter with the Other"—coming face to face with another human being and realizing that the Other is alive, looking at *you*, speaking to *you*, needing *you* to recognize him or her as someone who is fundamentally different from you and fundamentally vulnerable is the basis for all ethical thought and action.

If that person is gay, he or she is still the "other." For Levinas, the "other" was to be considered "better" than ourselves, not simple equal to us.[17] If that sounds radical, consider something even more radical—the "philosophy" of Matthew 25: "Truly I tell you, just as you did not do it to one of the least of these, you did not do it to me." In other words, how you treat others *is* how you treat Jesus.

Perhaps what we need in the church now is not a "revival" so much as a "reclamation." We have lost our soul by falling on the sword of our own fear and hatred. We are the Good Friday crowd masquerading as Easter people. We have forgotten where we came from, where we are going, and to Whom we belong. With our lips we say "life," but with our politics we peddle death.

Shame on us.

When you favor the death penalty and yet claim to be a follower of Jesus, who said an eye for an eye was the old way, not the way of the Kingdom, you are doing something immoral.

Even though support for the death penalty is eroding across the country, it still enjoys the strongest support among religious conservatives.[18] How can this be? State-sponsored killing as a form of punishment violates the soul of the Gospel itself, not to mention common sense. Those who are "pro-life" but also pro–death penalty mean to protect innocent prenatal life but not guilty postnatal life. Since it is impossible to commit a crime in the womb, the Christian Right is really saying that innocent life is sacred but guilty life is not—which is exactly the same thing as saying that not all life is sacred!

The real confusion in the death penalty debate is over the difference between vengeance and justice. In the strict father model of morality, children must be punished appropriately, or they will be encouraged to misbehave. Punishment that does not "fit the crime" encourages more crime. So when it comes to the death penalty, the ultimate crime deserves the ultimate punishment—even more so if it is particularly heinous. Who could argue, after all, on behalf of mass murderers like Timothy McVeigh, for example, who killed 168 of my friends and neighbors in Oklahoma City?

What's more, there is ample support in the Old Testament for killing as a form of punishment, including the infamous "eye for an eye" passage and the more direct "Whoever takes the life of any human being shall be put to death" (Leviticus 24:17). If you already believe in the death penalty, or think that you do, then lifting these passages out of context is convenient and preferable to studying them in their historical and cultural context.

For starters, "an eye for an eye" may be the most misunderstood passage in the Bible. Most scholars believe that it is not a formula for reciprocal violence but a way to actually limit violence by reducing its escalation. The text calls for "proportional retribution." In ancient Palestine, an offense against one's honor could be met with a disproportional response. If someone stole one of your sheep, you were permitted to respond by killing five of his cows. That would teach the appropriate lesson and restore your honor.

The "eye for an eye" ethic was an attempt to put a lid on such a disproportional response and the escalating violence that it encourages. Thus it was actually a move in the direction of restraint and moral progress.[19] For this reason, it is particularly astonishing that Jesus of Nazareth would cite this passage directly for reinterpretation: "You have heard it said, 'An eye for an eye and a tooth for a tooth.' But I say to you, Do not resist an evildoer. But if anyone strikes you on the right cheek, turn the other also; and if anyone wants to sue you and take your coat, give your cloak as well; and if anyone forces you to go one mile, go also the second mile" (Matthew 5:38–41).

While an eye for an eye was meant to restrain excessive punishments that were aimed at making "an example" out of criminals, Jesus goes even further by teaching that no form of retributive justice is acceptable. *An offense shall not be met with another offense.* Instead of feeling justified in a proportional response, you should make the opposite kind of disproportional response: if you lose your coat, give up you cloak as well.

This radical move, from retributive to restorative justice, indicts the direction that "America the punitive" has been moving. By passing a flood of "get-tough" laws like "three strikes and you're out," some punishments are now so disproportionate to some crimes that we have actually *reversed* the sentiments of an "eye for an eye." As prison populations have exploded and private prisons operate for profit by housing "clients," stories about ridiculous sentences abound. "In a 1994 case, a 14-year-old boy faced life in prison for selling $40 worth of marijuana to a schoolmate."[20]

The fact that we incarcerate more human beings, per capita, than any other nation on earth is shameful enough. But the fact that we remain one of the few nations on earth that kills people for killing people betrays any claim we might have to being Christian at all.

To begin with, religious arguments notwithstanding, the death penalty delivers on none of its promises. It does not deter crime, bring "closure" to victim's families, or cost less than a sentence of life without parole. We also know that innocent people have been executed and will be executed, and this fact alone has convinced many people that the death penalty should be abolished. That we have to struggle to outlaw the execution of juveniles is downright barbaric.

The strangest thing about the strong support for the death penalty in America is that it comes not from secular humanists, who have largely rejected it on logical grounds, but from religious conservatives who embrace it as God's command. To do so not only ignores the teachings of Jesus (who stopped an execution in progress when he spared the woman caught in adultery) but also betrays the oldest myth in the primitive religious mind: that *violence saves*.

An ancient Babylonian Creation story, older than the Bible itself, describes a rebellion among the gods, in which Marduk kills the mother god, Tiamat, and then stretches out her corpse to create the cosmos. The message is clear, and we still live by it: violence is our origin; war brings peace, death brings life. It is the Roman recipe that "might makes right" and that it is better to be feared than to be loved. We live by this creed—in literature, in the movies, and in our public policy. We like to say that Jesus saves, but down deep we believe that violence saves.[21]

This tension, between the belief that violence saves, on the one hand, and that only the end of violence can save us, on the other, runs through human history from the beginning of time to the present day. Religious traditions oppose violence at first, and their followers take up the ways of nonviolence. But inevitably those same followers end up resorting to violence again, believing that for the sake of preserving their particular version of the truth, some people must die. A God of Love is revealed to us, again and again, and yet we continue to kill for that God because we have not yet left all traces of Marduk behind.

Several years ago, I had a life-changing experience when I met and became spiritual adviser to Wanda Jean Allen, the first woman executed by the state of Oklahoma. The case drew national attention and became the subject of an award-winning HBO documentary titled *The Execution of Wanda Jean*. Perhaps in no other single death penalty case has all that's wrong with the death penalty come into such sharp and tragic focus.

Her attorney, who is a member of my congregation, asked me to present her appeal for clemency. This unusual decision was motivated by two factors. First, that no other clemency approach had ever worked, so we had nothing to lose. And second, that since clemency is an appeal for *mercy*, not a retrying of the case, who better to argue for mercy than a minister? And where better to do it than in Oklahoma, where the name of Jesus ranks right up there with country and western singers and Sooner quarterbacks?

Wanda Jean Allen was born into the most dysfunctional family I have ever seen. She was poor, black, female, lesbian, brain-damaged, and mentally retarded. A childhood accident had left her with a long scar down the side of head and damage to her brain's frontal lobe—the part of the brain that checks violent impulses. She dropped out of school in the ninth grade and disappeared into a world of pimps, prostitutes, drugs, and guns. Before she ended up on death row, she killed twice—a woman outside a bar in Tulsa and then a woman she met in prison, Gloria Leathers, after a bitter and violent breakup.

Her attorney had never tried a capital case and begged to be excused, but the judge refused. So for $800 and with no help from the state, Wanda Jean was "defended" against the death penalty by a man who did not even make the jury aware of her mental illness and retardation. She was on death row for thirteen years, where she became deeply religious and well liked in the prison community. When I would visit her, along with her attorneys, she would lead us in prayer. Her Bible was marked up on every page, and she could quote more Scripture than most clergy I know. Ironically, the structured world of prison had given her a better life than she had had on the street. All she wanted was to live in that prison until she died.

When I presented the case for clemency to the Pardon and Parole Board, it was an exercise in futility. In particular, the state expressed resentment at the idea that an ordained minister should even lead the appeal. "God has no place in this clemency hearing," said the spokesman for the attorney general. When it was over, the vote was 5–1 to deny clemency, and Wanda Jean was executed a few weeks later.

In many ways, my experience paralleled that of Sister Helen Prejean, who wrote *Dead Man Walking*, and the lessons I learned about the death penalty in America are no longer just intellectual for me but visceral. The poor get one form of justice, the rich another, and in Oklahoma, a poor, black, brain-damaged lesbian has no chance of getting the same sympathy that a jury might have extended to a straight, white woman. To exploit the jury's homophobia, the state went to great lengths in the trial to prove that Wanda Jean Allen "killed like a man."

But of all the bitter ironies, none could compare with the religious hypocrisy. The state sought to persuade us that we were killing the same woman who had killed thirteen years ago, not the Wanda Jean Allen who had become a model prisoner, led Bible study, and was well liked by the other inmates. Granted, there are last-minute religious conversions in prison, but this wasn't case with Wanda Jean. So why would the state of Oklahoma, one of the most publicly "Christian" places on earth, scoff at the idea that faith might actually *change* a person? If not, then what is religion for?

When they scolded me for bringing God into the clemency hearing, I thought to myself, we are not allowed to use religious arguments in a state-run prison while trying to decide whether or not to *kill* someone, but we can insist that the Ten Commandments be posted on every schoolhouse wall, one of which says, "Thou shall not kill."

The truth is that we want God when God serves *our* purposes but not when God doesn't. To add insult to death, the state kicked God out of the clemency hearing but then brought God back for the execution. As a witness to the execution, I watched the lethal cocktail of drugs flow through tubes from behind a wall and into Wanda Jean's veins. Standing beside her was a state prison chaplain, reading passages of Scripture aloud to Wanda Jean as the state was killing her!

Just think about this. God could not be in the room when we contemplated mercy but was invited back into the death chamber to comfort the one to whom we had refused it. When asked to make a final statement, she raised her head and said this into the microphone: "Father forgive them, for they know not what they do."

As to that mythical construct "closure," something quite remarkable happened at the clemency hearing. Not a single member of the victim's family asked the state to kill Wanda Jean, reminding us all that it wouldn't bring back their loved one. They simply asked that she never leave prison so that she could never kill again. So in the end, nobody in the room wanted Wanda Jean Allen dead *except* the state of Oklahoma.

Consider the irony here. The state that insisted on killing Wanda Jean is the state that wants a constitutional amendment to allow mandatory school prayer. It favors faith-based initiatives to allow tax dollars to help spread the Gospel. We finally got around to outlawing the blood sport of cockfighting, but not without a fight. Then an Oklahoma legislator suggested bringing it back, but in a kinder, gentler form—by putting tiny boxing gloves on the roosters.

In Oklahoma, owning a gun is a divine right. And when Oral Roberts wanted to raise more money once, he warned his followers that God would "call him home" (take his life) if they did not send him a sufficient sum. This may have been a first in fundraising circles—asking people to contribute money in order placate a potential Divine Assassin. It would be funny, if it weren't so sad—and so dangerous.

We say we hate violence in this country, but that's not true. We love it.

It all adds up to Marduk.

Violence saves.

Chapter Seven

"Pro-Life" Should
Include Mother Nature

When you dismantle countless environmental laws designed to protect the earth, which is God's gift to us all, so that the corporations that bought you and paid for your favors will make higher profits while our children breathe dirty air and live in a toxic world, you have done something immoral. The earth belongs to the Lord, not Halliburton.

This ought to be the one issue that everyone can agree on. Even in these fractured times, this ought to be a nonpartisan "no-brainer." In fact, when it comes to the environment, we should all be "conservatives," committed to *conserving* the planet we live on. This fragile lifeboat is sinking under the weight of six billion people and counting, warmed by greenhouse gases that we create and then dump into the atmospheric equivalent of a landfill. There is a growing hole in the ozone layer, putting every single person exposed to sunlight at risk of getting skin cancer. The polar ice caps are melting, glaciers are receding, and ocean temperatures are rising and feeding stronger hurricanes. Ten of the hottest years in recorded history have occurred since 1980. Countless species have vanished, fish populations are shrinking, and coral reefs are disappearing. We stand on the precipice of a global disaster, and the official response of the United States is arrogant denial.[1]

When President George W. Bush withdrew American support for the Kyoto Protocol, he sent the world a message about our priorities and our willingness to sacrifice for the rest of the humankind. With only 5 percent of the population, we use 25 percent of the world's resources while producing more trash and pollution than any other nation. Therefore, our participation was crucial, both in substance, and symbolically.

"The earth belongs to the LORD, and the fullness thereof," begins the Twenty-Fourth Psalm. There may be no single issue in our time that more fully reveals one's true religious sentiment, or lack thereof, than one's approach to the environment. A true environmentalist takes the long view and works on behalf of generations yet unborn. Antienvironmentalists, who are often professing Christians, regard short-term benefits (especially short-term profits) as more important than long-term consequences. Sadly, the old texts that counseled us to "be fruitful and multiply" or "have dominion over the earth and subdue it" were written at a time when human survival was the issue and humans regarded the earth as an enemy to be conquered. But the roots of our separation from the earth run deeper.

When our ancestors in faith, the Hebrews, conquered the Canaanites, they regarded it as not only a human victory but also a vindication of the male sky god over the fertility goddess Astarte and her male consort Baal. Instead of regarding the earth as something sacred, it was regarded as something to be conquered—before it conquered us. When Christianity followed Judaism, this same "antiearth" attitude prevailed. As Bishop Spong put it:

> Jesus was understood as one who had invaded the earth on behalf of or at the behest of the Father God from the sky. The religion that developed into Christianity encouraged its worshipers to dream of and to anticipate the real life that would occur in heaven and thus not to focus their attention on this earth or to have any responsibility for its care, its nurture, or its transformation. Salvation was portrayed as escaping the earth, which was somehow evil. It was a human-centered but heavenward-bound emphasis. Ecological disaster was all but inevitable.[2]

Even as the world develops a new global consciousness or recovers some of the most ancient holistic ideas about the sacredness of Creation, it is the West that fights back and continues to see Mother Nature as something that needs to be controlled by Father God. Indeed, the strict father model of morality often fears what it cannot control and regards the earth's mysterious fertility and capricious violence as "fickle," "tempestuous," even "profligate" in its capacity to give life and take it away. The earth seems in one moment to be peaceful, pastoral, and maternal, only to turn suddenly wicked, as when tsunamis sweep away sleeping children and earthquakes drop overpasses on unsuspecting commuters and crush them to death. What was their "sin"? Being in the wrong place at the wrong time?

Thus it is no accident that our relationship to nature in the Abrahamic religious traditions so closely mirrors our understanding of how men ought to treat women. It is, after all, common male wisdom that what is not "subdued" will make a fool of you. The truth is, however, that the earth is now in the process of making a fool of all of us. Because everything really is connected to everything else, as the mystics have long understood, and quantum physics is now confirming, we are fast approaching a point of no return. Just as the human body cannot sustain being out of balance too long before it mutates, the body of the earth itself is on the verge of getting "cancer"—an uncontrollable mutation of the ecosystem. The symptoms are already apparent, and the treatments can be successful only if they begin at once and are globally "aggressive."

Greenhouse gases must be drastically cut, toxic pollutants must be eliminated, rivers and streams must return to their natural state and not be dammed, nonbiodegradable items must be recycled, and agriculture must adopt organic methods. This needs to happen not because of any particular political ideology but so that the human race can survive. The "healing" of the planet must begin *now*, and it's going to take a long, long time.

We will have to look beyond the next quarterly profit report and adopt the "long view" that is truly religious. After all, the horizon is not the end of things but merely the limit of our sight. Patience is not just a virtue. It is a manifestation of true faith. As

Luther put it in his great hymn, "A thousand ages in thy sight / Are like an evening gone, / Short as the watch that ends the night / Before the rising sun."

This would take courageous leadership, of course, a call for mutual sacrifice, and a shared vision because "Where there is no vision, the people perish" (Proverbs 29:18). So why is it that the most overtly "religious" president in the modern era has presided over what both Democrats and Republicans call "the most antienvironmental administration in U.S. history"?[3] Under his leadership as governor of Texas, the Environmental Protection Agency declared that state "the most polluted in the country." Now, despite the stealth doublespeak of "Clear Skies" and "Healthy Forests" legislation, Bush has put notorious polluters in charge of protecting America from pollution. When Michael Leavitt replaced Christine Whitman as head of the EPA, one of his first acts was to dismantle President Clinton's mercury rule, even though fish in forty-eight states are now unsafe to eat. Today, one out of every six American women has so much mercury in her womb that her children are at risk for a long list of grim diseases.[4] Is this what it means to be "pro-life"?

The sad truth is that Washington, D.C., has now become a giant corporate lobbying farm that has nothing whatsoever to do with deliberative democracy. Public service used to be about putting the common good ahead of private ambition, but "we the people" cannot begin to compete with the power of special interests. What's more, we can hardly compete with God. The appointment and reelection of George W. Bush was called an "act of God" by leading preachers on the Right. Among them, the president of Bob Jones University wrote an open letter to the president, saying, in part, "God has graciously granted America—though she doesn't deserve it—a reprieve from the agenda of paganism."[5]

It would be more accurate to say that this "victory" is not one of good over evil but of money over a résumé. The president has lots of people to pay back, and his constituency regards the earth as a source of capital, not as a sacred trust. Environmental laws cut into profits, and profits are what we worship. Creation itself is seen by countless capitalists as a vast inventory of raw materials, not a derivative of grace.

The Bush record on the environment is as dismal as its consequences are disastrous. For a Congress that flaunts its religiosity, what is faithful about gutting key provisions of the Clean Water and Clean Air acts, which have done more to protect the health of Americans than any other environmental legislation? What is "Christian" about crippling the Superfund program, which cleans up toxic waste sites in neighborhoods all over America? What is "moral" about weakening the enforcement division of the EPA, making it less effective, and giving it less authority to regulate polluters? Fines and prosecutions are at an all-time low.

This is the first administration ever not to voluntarily add a single species to the endangered species list, and it has opened more public land to logging, mining, and oil and gas exploration than any other. After promising in his campaign debate with Al Gore that global warming was something that "needs to be taken very seriously," Bush did an about face and said he would not regulate CO_2 emissions from factories that contribute one-fourth of the world's total carbon particulate pollution.6

If scientific reports conflict with the administration's probusiness, antienvironmental agenda, they are purged or censored. That charge has come increasingly from concerned scientists, including twenty Nobel laureates, leading medical experts, and former federal agency directors who met in Washington, D.C., recently to call for "regulatory and legislative action to restore scientific integrity to federal policymaking."7

Jesus may be the most important person in the president's life, but he certainly doesn't pick his cabinet the way the Lord picked his disciples. The former asks men to leave their old lives and, in service to others, give up everything to walk into new ones. The latter asks men to leave their old private sector jobs and become the public sector regulators of their own industry. After they retire (or are fired for incompetence), they become consultants or lobbyists for the private sector again, but now with an insider's view of government regulation. This revolving-door policy is fantastically lucrative, but it puts the fox in charge of the henhouse.

The ironies don't stop there. Mountaintops are holy places in Scripture. Moses goes up on a mountain to receive the law and the commandments, and Jesus does the same to pray and to be transfigured. "I lift up my eyes to the hills—from where will my help come? My help comes from the LORD, who made heaven and earth," says Psalm 121.

For the Bush administration, however, there is something more valuable than wisdom in those hills. It has given the green light to mountaintop removal as a form of mining. This involves blasting away entire mountaintops in complex ecosystems like Appalachia and dumping the resulting rubble, called spoil, into the adjacent valleys. The practice has already buried miles of streams and destroyed tens of thousands of acres of woodlands. To speed up the process, the administration reduced existing regulations and streamlined the process of getting mining permits.[8]

When Vice President Dick Cheney met secretly with leaders of the energy industry to formulate the nation's energy policy in the spring of 2001, the real agenda was oil, and the documents eventually turned over as part of various Freedom of Information Act lawsuits revealed detailed maps of Iraqi oilfields, pipelines, refineries, and terminals. One was labeled "Foreign Suitors for Iraqi Oilfield Contracts." The struggle to keep those meetings secret so that the administration could get "unvarnished advice" has led to speculation that the seeds of the invasion of Iraq were sown long before 9/11.

We may never know the truth about what happened in those meetings, but one thing is certain. The private-public policy collusion has become seamless and secretive. If the public does not have the right to know how public energy policy was drafted by a public official at public expense, then what has become of "public service"? The truth is that we are not "represented" by our elected officials so much as we send them to Washington to be lobbied and then assess them based on whether they caved in to the right constituencies!

This is more than just a civics problem. It is deeply rooted in the religious convictions of the Christian Right—a strict father government acting on behalf of a strict Father God—and Father knows best. Just follow the money. If environmentalists contributed more money to political campaigns than the mining, timber, and energy companies, we would see more environmental protection. Until that happens, or until we enact real campaign finance reform, the environment will continue to be "subdued."

Hurricane Katrina was a wake-up call. Not only did it expose the tragic consequences of precious resources diverted to the hopeless war in Iraq, but it also reminded us that if we mistreat the natural world, Mother Nature will have the last word. The dams and levees we have built to keep rivers from flooding have also stopped the natural process of silt deposits that make and replenish wetlands. Those wetlands not only spawn life and preserve it but also act as a buffer to "absorb" hurricanes as they make landfall. Draining the swamp and building on the sand is, as ancient Scripture teach us, a recipe for disaster.

Episcopal priest Matthew Fox wrote a controversial book in the 1980s called *The Coming of the Cosmic Christ,* in which he argues for the return of a Creation-centered mysticism in the church, lest we kill our own Mother. Fox had a vivid dream, what Native Americans call a "big dream," in which the dominant image was of a kind of environmental matricide: *Your Mother Is Dying.*[9] The way we treat the earth, Fox tells us, is like a cosmic template for the way we treat one another. The death of compassion brings the death of hope, of children, of native peoples, their cultures, and their religious wisdom. As the Mother dies, so die all her children.

More revealing still is Fox's contention that when true mysticism is absent, a true "cosmology" is absent as well—that is, an awareness of one's place in the universe. When this happens, people substitute what he calls "pseudomysticisms" to fill the void, such as "fundamentalisms" of all kinds (religious or ideological), and all manner of addictions. Not knowing our cosmic place means that we are like spiritual orphans, perpetually striving to locate ourselves as the children of *might* (militarism), of *altered consciousness* (drugs and alcohol), or of *fame and fortune* (what Fox calls our brain-numbing worship of popular celebrities). We either become religious fanatics, kill, drop out, or find our fifteen seconds of fame. The ultimate perversion of religion, therefore, would be to turn the founder of Christian mysticism, Jesus of Nazareth, into just another celebrity!

Fox reminds us that we have largely lost our own mystical tradition or no longer trust that it will not degenerate into New Age nonsense. Many conservative Christians were warned that *mysticism* "begins with mist, centers on 'I,' and ends in schism."[10] For Protestants, it sounds vaguely medieval and suspiciously Roman Catholic. Mystics as a class were regarded as withdrawn, eccentric, and fatiguing in their otherworldliness. But Fox argues that we are all mystics, unaware, because we have all had experiences of the transcendent.

His favorite example is the astronaut Rusty Schweikert, who found himself stranded outside his *Apollo* capsule high above the earth in 1969. Floating in complete silence, this left-brained, nonemotive macho fighter pilot had an epiphany when he gazed back at the earth, "like a shining gem against a totally black backdrop." He was so overcome by what he saw that he wanted to "hug and kiss that gem like a mother does her firstborn child." That would be a strange thing to say to ground control, of course. "Houston, I need a little time alone." Lucky for us, there are poets like Archibald MacLeish to say what Schweikert could not say. "To see the earth as we now see it, small and beautiful in that eternal silence where it floats, is to see ourselves as riders on the earth together."[11]

From that vantage point, there are no political divisions, no borders to stop rivers, no trade zones in the clouds. Tolstoy had the same vision without going into space: *there are no nations*. There is only Creation and the delicate balance that sustains it all. While scholars still debate the historical Jesus, which is vitally important, Fox hails the need for a Cosmic Christ—a savior who can connect us to the divine order by having stood between the disorder and brutality of the cross and the redemptive power and mystery of a God who appears to abandon him, and all of us, but in fact has called us home. Home to our essential unity. Home to our connection to everything—to the animals (who surrounded Christ at his birth), the sick, the outcast, the forgotten, the weak.

This is not the Warrior Christ of our violent culture but the Cosmic Christ of a new global consciousness, the "firstborn of all creation. . . . In him were created all things in heaven and earth: everything visible and invisible. . . . He holds all things in unity," as the letter to the Colossians (1:15–17) puts it. Or when we read in the letter to the Philippians that at the name of Jesus "every knee should bow in heaven and earth and under the earth" (2:10), the message is not one of obligatory conversion or fearful obedience but rather a hymn of universal acclamation.

Against this cosmic consciousness, consider again the dismissive, impatient, ethnocentric rhetoric of this "born-again" administration. The world is either with us or against us. The coalition is either willing or unwilling (and thus irrelevant). The Arctic Wildlife Refuge either produces oil and gas or is essentially useless. Trade is either "free" or unfair. People either "love freedom" or they "hate our way of life." This us-against-them mentality is the opposite of the Cosmic Christ. It is antiredemptive and thus irreligious. It is the sickness of our time, what Fox calls a truncated, anthropocentric "personal savior Christianity."

Calling us to a "deep ecumenism" that counters the Enlightenment emphasis on the individual and Newton's desacralized, machinelike universe, Fox long ago sounded the call to what he calls the "greening of the Religious Life." We will have to reconsider our cosmology in a painful way and take instruction about care of the earth from sources we once considered primitive and superstitious. After all, Mother Earth is dying before our eyes.

For this reason, our mysticism cannot be simply personal and private. We may learn the disciplines of connecting to the divine in nature again, but this does not free us from considering the consequences of public policy. If the church is to recover its soul, it must be committed to *social* mysticism. The artificial disconnect between "religion and politics," which plagues the church today, is not about *whether* they are connected but *how* they are connected. The first person to tell a preacher to stay out of politics, after all, was the pharaoh, who insisted that Moses tend to the spiritual well-being of his people and leave revolutions to the politicians.

There are hopeful signs that our own green revolution is coming, even if the signs are often as deadly as they are obvious. The planet itself is giving us powerful evidence that it has had enough and will now fight back. We will need not only a new cosmology if we are to survive but a new theology as well. The historic understanding of God as a supernatural being who lives outside of Creation but periodically invades the world to reward or punish his creatures is called *theism*. For many people, this notion of God has become as meaningless as it is illogical. They have rejected both the notion of God as Puppeteer and Jesus as Alien. But they have not given up on faith. Their numbers are legion, and they beg for a second chance to believe and to be transformed.

What we do not believe is that heaven is our home. We believe that *this* is our home and the abode of the sacred. We believe that *this* is the world that Jesus came to redeem and that *these* are the people he came to save. If we look past each other, to some future reward, we lose everything. If we ignore the groans of this planet because we think we are soon to leave it, we are in childish denial and are dooming future generations to unspeakable suffering. Because compassion is the essence of faith, we have to be very careful not to condone bad theology. An absentee landlord God will produce absentee tenant followers who will pay one month's rent, stay a month and a half, and then move in the night.

The Bible does not have a single way of conceiving of God, and we will have to continue the evolution away from theism and toward an understanding of God as the breath of life, the mysterious, animating spirit that is closer to what theologian Paul Tillich called the "ground of being." If not, we will continue to worship a partisan God who will encourage partisan followers to interact with the earth and each other in a partisan way. If we believe that God plays favorites, we will feel justified in doing the same. We will continue to see the earth as a warehouse, not as a sacred endowment. We will go on polluting the air, poisoning the rivers, and cutting down the forests because we want what we want *now*. But however we justify it, let's not confuse it with faith.

One cannot claim to be "pro-life" if one is complicit in the death of one's Mother.

Chapter Eight

We Have Met the Enemy

When you claim that our God is bigger than their God and that
our killing is righteous while theirs is evil, we have begun to
resemble the enemy we claim to be fighting, and that is immoral. We have met the enemy, and the enemy is us.

It was a comic strip hero named Pogo who gave us the perfect phrase
for describing blind hypocrisy: "We have met the enemy and he is
us." Lest we forget, the very term *enemy* is itself a construct of the
nonenemy, and a very useful one at that. There has been more talk
lately of *evil* and *enemies* than ever before. The president's Mani-
chaean worldview is constantly on display, and the view from his
bully pulpit is a world neatly divided between good and evil, like a
giant rhetorical machete dropped on a planetary watermelon. Ca-
thump! The cut is swift and clean. The halves roll apart. One half
is sweet, the other is rotten, and nobody has to guess which one is
America. We are the heart and soul of the "axis of good."

When lumping the Iraqi insurgents together with the terrorists
of 9/11, the president said that they are all "enemies of civilization"
and share "a fanatical political ideology."

That certainly describes the hijackers, but it does not describe
every Iraqi nationalist who wants to expel an occupying army from
his own country. They have met the enemy, and the enemy is us.

It would be one thing if the president and his Christian Right
defenders simply ignored the double standard of calling all "enemy"

resistance an "insurgency" while calling our eighteenth-century re-sistance to British occupation, for example, "patriotic." Or more recently, to call the rebels we armed against the Sandinistas in Ni-caragua "freedom fighters." Just as there are no Israeli "terrorists," there are also no American "insurgents." Our resistance, regardless of tactics, is always an act of bravery. The resistance of those we oc-cupy is always an act of barbarism. Yet we, of all people, ought to un-derstand the universal power of our own revolutionary motto: DON'T TREAD ON ME. There is no force in nature quite so powerful as the response of human beings to occupation by a foreign power.

But there is something even more serious going on here than a double standard or linguistic duplicity. What's happening in the world, we are told, is part of a cosmic struggle of good versus evil, and through regrettable, it is *unavoidable*. Real men understand this, and liberals don't, because they follow the nurturant parent model of morality. A strict father who uses corporal punishment, for example, tells the child he is about to spank, "This is for your own good," or more incredible, "This is going to hurt me more than it hurts you."

President Bush takes much the same approach when he lectures us on his tough-love response to a big, bad world, telling us repeatedly that without cosmic pain, there is no cosmic gain. Just as misbehav-ing children cannot be coddled, neither can misbehaving nations. In the fundamentalist mind, leniency encourages depravity, while the rod of swift discipline clarifies and purifies. With a wink and a nod, this strict father president is doing what *must be done*—what he be-lieves a wrathful God wants him to do. Spare the rod and spoil the terrorist.

If anyone still doubts that Bush is on a holy mission, just listen to the president's own words during a televised press conference: "I also have this belief, strong belief, that freedom is not this country's gift to the world; freedom is the Almighty's gift to every man and woman in this world. And as the greatest power on the face of the earth, we have an obligation to help the spread of freedom."[1]

The argument here is unmistakable. Major premise: God wants freedom for everyone. Minor premise: We are the greatest power on earth. Implied premise: God can't do it alone but requires help from the strongest nation. Conclusion: Therefore, we have an obligation to help God spread freedom.

This is exactly the same thing as saying, "We are doing God's work by invading and occupying Iraq, because God needs our help to spread freedom and democracy throughout the world." By this rationale, any invasion we deemed necessary to spread freedom and democracy would have God's blessing. No wonder the rest of the world sees this as a religious crusade (or an oil grab masquerading as a crusade). We have mixed arrogance with absolutism, and the result is that we are conducting our own "jihad" (in the perverted sense of the word) and fueling the very hatred we claim to be fighting.

If the noblest act of a Christian is to forgive one's enemies and pray for them, then what do we call the act of *creating* even more enemies in order to justify becoming the world's leading exporter of violence? Is it not true that since the beginning of our republic, we have destabilized or destroyed countless governments we did not like, supported insurgencies and counterinsurgencies to achieve our objectives, and become the world's largest arms dealer? In the name of "national security" we have spread death from our own western frontier to Central America to East Timor. For most of the twentieth century, Soviet communism gave us the perfect enemy in a neatly "bipolar" world. We fought a political war on countless "borrowed" battlefields. We knew what we *were* because we knew what we were *not*.

After the Berlin Wall came down and the USSR imploded, we moved quickly to create a new "enemy," which we called "rogue states"—Iraq, Libya, Cuba, and North Korea for starters. In a 1995 document called *Essentials of Post–Cold War Deterrence*, the American military establishment sought to move beyond Cold War strategies of mutual assured destruction and control rogue states. We did this by making it clear that we were willing to use nuclear weapons to respond to any threats from all adversaries. Resurrecting President Richard Nixon's "madman theory," the new strategy emphasizes that we should appear potentially "out of control" so that our "enemies" would see us as "crazed and unpredictable."[2] Rationality was seen as a weakness and did not engender sufficient fear in the enemy. Forget "blessed are the peacemakers."

What is and is not a "rogue state" is constantly shifting, of course, just as Eurasia and Eastasia are interchangeable "enemies" in George Orwell's 1984. It does not matter which one we are fighting, only that warfare is continuous and accomplishes its primary objective according to the principle of *doublethink*, "to use up the products of the machine without raising the general standard of living." It also keeps the average person in a state of continuous "fear, hatred, adulation, and orgiastic triumph." In what may yet turn out to be the most prophetic book written in the twentieth century, Orwell's Emmanuel Goldstein explains one of the three defining paradoxes of doublethink (WAR IS PEACE) with words that could be taken from our morning newspaper:

> It does not matter whether the war is actually happening, and, since no decisive victory is possible, it does not matter whether the war is going well or badly. All that is needed is that a state of war should exist. . . . It is precisely in the Inner Party that war hysteria and hatred of the enemy are strongest. In his capacity as an administrator, it is often necessary for a member of the Inner Party to know that this or that item of war news is untruthful, and is either not happening or is being waged for purposes quite other than the declared ones; but such knowledge is easily neutralized by the technique of "doublethink." Meanwhile no Inner Party member wavers for an instant in his mystical belief that the war *is* real, and that it is bound to end victoriously, with Oceania the undisputed master of the entire world.[3]

This ability, to hold two inherently contradictory thoughts in one's mind simultaneously without feeling what psychologists call "cognitive dissonance," is the essence of doublethink. For Bush and his military establishment, however, there is an added element that is considerably more frightening: our war is God's war. How do we know this? Because the top soldier assigned the task of tracking down and eliminating Osama bin Laden, Saddam Hussein, and other high-profile terrorist targets put it plainly. Lieutenant General William G. "Jerry" Boykin, an outspoken evangelical Christian who often speaks in church in full uniform, declared that radical Islamists hate us "because we're a Christian nation, because our foundation and our roots are Judeo-Christian . . . and the enemy is a guy named Satan."[4]

As to the relationship between this worldview and violence, this is the same man who briefed a top Pentagon civilian official on how to interrogate Iraqi prisoners to "soften them up," thus helping set the stage for the shame of Abu Ghraib and Guantanamo Bay. The result has been a disaster for the United States and for our reputation with those whose "hearts and minds" we are trying to win.

In an increasingly familiar spectacle, the White House distanced itself from Boykin's views, reminding us that they are his "personal" views, and then allowed him to continue in his command and advise top government officials. This way, the "base" is gratified, and loyalty is rewarded. As for losing his job, that never happens in the Bush administration.

Boykin has said that Bush "was not elected by a majority of the voters—he was appointed by God." We can only defeat our enemies, he said, if "we come against them in the name of Jesus." After battling a Muslim warlord in Somalia, he said, "I knew my God was bigger than his. I knew that my God was a real God and his was an idol."[5]

There is perhaps no more inflammatory word to use in this situation than *idol*. For many Muslims, who believe that the "Judeo-Christian" world is at war with Islam, this is like throwing gasoline on a fire. Although the president has made numerous statements disavowing any intention to lead a "crusade" against the Muslim world and has called Islam a "religion of peace," the word on the Arab street is too often just the opposite.

When Lieutenant Colonel Gary Brandl was leading eight hundred soldiers in an all-out offensive against Fallujah, Iraq, he said, "The enemy has got a face. He's called Satan. He's in Fallujah, and we're going to destroy him."[6] Other comments left the impression that coalition forces who died were killed by Satan and that we now have a moral obligation to avenge not just their deaths by the enemy but also to chase down and eliminate the Devil himself. So what is the difference between that statement and many of those made by Osama bin Laden? Either way, it's a holy war mentality.

Despite all the publicity about Abu Ghraib and Guantanamo, and our obligatory condemnations, it would appear that only what is "caught on tape" is officially repugnant. In the fall of 2005, U.S. forces again disgraced both the American military and the Geneva Convention by burning the corpses of dead Taliban fighters and taunting their opponents over loudspeakers. They placed the bodies on the ground facing Mecca and then lit them on fire, calling the fighters "cowardly dogs" and "lady boys." On orders from their superiors in the Army psychological operations unit, they sought to maximize the humiliation of the enemy by mocking sacred Muslim burial practices and said, in Arabic, "You attack and run away like women."[7]

The next time our soldiers are publicly burned or beheaded in retaliation, we can expect the same response: see what evil we are up against? But with even more pictures now coming out of Abu Ghraib, the word *evil* is coming back to haunt us.

This "my God is bigger than your God" mentality is not just a product of human nature. It's a product of bad theology. The only way in which God will cease being co-opted for the purpose of violence is when we change our way of thinking about God. As long as we are trapped in biblical literalism, the theology of the Fall, and God's invasion from the sky to rescue some while letting others perish, violence in the name of God will never cease. We will have to reject the idea of a once-perfect Creation from which human beings could fall into sin, because a perfect Creation never existed and we continue to evolve.

In what theologians call process theology, Creation is not finished, and God is not "resting." We do not need a savior to "pay the price for our sins," as if God is a Cosmic Banker who requires innocent human collateral to balance the books. Until we shed the "shedding of blood" as the central metaphor of Christianity, the shedding of blood will continue.

Consider the stupendous success of Mel Gibson's movie *The Passion of the Christ*, which truncates the compassionate life of Jesus into one agonizingly long sadomasochistic spectacle glorifying a kind of cosmic child abuse. It is but one more warning shot across the bow of our culture. Even though it was rated R for violence (and graphic scenes of torture), devout parents took their young children to see the film, some as young as twelve. This violence was "holy," they told their children. It was what God wanted, and the world needs to be saved.

Now we stand at a crossroads in human history. The violence we think will save us cannot, and the evidence of the failure to be "protected" by either a righteous president or a partisan God is omnipresent. Despite the fact that evil cannot be controlled by threats or by "discipline," whether parental or divine, the name of the Prince of Peace is once more carrying soldiers into battle, this time to slay the dragon called terrorism. The result is the "downward spiral" that Martin Luther King Jr. described as inevitable. Fighting terrorism with divinely sanctioned violence is like hitting quicksilver with a ball-peen hammer.

Living in Oklahoma brings this bellicose brand of patriotism home just by turning on the radio and listening to country music. Wrapped in the flag and cheered by millions as a role model to our children, country singer Toby Keith captured the mood of so many after the attacks of 9/11. In a wildly popular song called "Courtesy of the Red, White, and Blue," he taught his adoring fans that vengeance is as American as apple pie.

We are not violent by nature, of course, but we're like a sleeping giant that must never be roused or a "big dog" whose bark is peace but whose bite is fearsome and deadly. Just to make it clear what happens if you mess with the U.S.A., Keith sings, "We'll put a boot in your ass / It's the American way." With friends like this, who needs enemies? With a God like this, who needs Patton?

❖

> When you tell people that you intend to run and govern as
> a "compassionate conservative," using a word that is the
> essence of all religious faith—*compassion*—and then show
> no compassion for anyone who disagrees with you and no
> patience with those who cry to you for help, you are doing
> something immoral.

The Republican Party has an "image problem" when it comes to the poor. Most of the party leaders are wealthy white males who hate welfare "giveaways" to the poor but love government "partnerships" in the form of tax breaks and other "incentives" for corporations. They do not oppose government spending to help businesses. They oppose government spending to ease poverty. The former is good for business, and a rising tide floats all boats, they tell us. The latter is a "plantation mentality" by which Democrats actually enslave the poor and keep them dependent and irresponsible.

Because this idea is so firmly established in the public mind, and many Americans believe that Republicans care only about the rich, conservatives are often quick to point out how religious they are and how much they believe in the charitable work of faith communities. In fact, they would like to see private charity largely replace public assistance as the principal means of helping the poor, even if it means giving public money directly to private charities through so-called faith-based initiatives. Never mind that this violates the separation of church and state. Many who run the country now do not believe in such separation. One right-wing TV preacher, Rod Parsley, calls the separation of church and state "a lie perpetrated on Americans—especially believers in Jesus Christ."[8] Not all traditional Republicans share this crusading mentality, but there is an actual bumper sticker that proclaims the GOP to be "God's Own Party." And moderates have so far been willing to put up with such nonsense if it wins them more power. They take the votes and turn away from the obvious danger because the two political agendas are now in bed together.

Some moderates, however, are beginning to get worried. Episcopal priest and former Republican Senator John Danforth wrote a powerful op-ed piece in the *New York Times* that began, "By a series of recent initiatives, Republicans have transformed our party into the political arm of conservative Christians."[9] Jim Wallis took the warning a step further, saying that "some Religious Right leaders are trying to transform the church into the religious arm of conservative Republicans. Either way, these partisan attempts to hijack faith and politics are wrong."[10]

How do they get away with this? It's very simple. Because "self-help" is the basis for the strict father morality model, the government should not run "programs" that assist the poor (which only rewards lack of discipline) but should create "pathways" to greater opportunity. The way to help the poor is to help the rich so that the rich can provide the poor with more job opportunities and then get out of the way. Individuals who fall on hard times should join a church, visit a homeless shelter, or find a private charitable organization that can help them "get back on their feet." Government has more urgent work to do, like fighting wars and building new football and baseball stadiums in major cities.

To counteract this image problem, the choreographers of the Bush campaign created something quite wonderful, a hitherto unknown political creature called a "compassionate conservative." George W. Bush ran for president as a bridge-building moderate who would "do business in a new way in Washington." Despite the pleasing alliteration of "compassionate conservative," it sounded strange, like an oxymoron, as if perhaps he meant to redefine what conservatism is all about. Perhaps, the voters thought, he might actually combine the limited government sensibilities of traditional Republicans with an appropriate amount of compassion for the poor? That is, maybe he could do *both*—be a conservative and a liberal, a strict father with a soft side. As it turned out, the phrase was merely invented for the campaign, like his father's "thousand points of light," and then put away forever, just like the mock indignation over gay marriage.

The important thing in politics these days is to sound sincere and appear to be kind and caring, even if your policies result in more poverty, more pain, and more people living without health insurance or hope. As the Danish philosopher Søren Kierkegaard pointed out, there is a profound difference between concept and capacity. One does not become gracious by reading a good book on grace. Thinking good thoughts or saying good things does not make you a good person. Or to put it biblically, "By their fruits you shall know them" (Matthew 7:16).

The astonishing disconnect between rhetoric and reality in this administration is identical to the disconnect in the American church between pulpit pronouncements and the mission budget. We regard the idea of love very highly but seem unwilling to sacrifice much for it. Members pledge what's left over to the church budget, and then the church pledges what left over in the budget to help the poor— so that our mission dollars are what's left over from what's left over!

What's more, we love to talk about "freedom" in church, but that concept has now also been hijacked. The old idea of "freedom in Christ" did not mean every man or woman for himself or herself. It meant the freedom to voluntarily enter into even deeper levels of covenant, community, and mutuality. We answered this question long ago: we *are* our brother's and sister's keeper, not just their competition. Our government is therefore *not* the enemy from which we must be freed but the collective conscience that we elect and empower to serve us and protect us.

When the Christian Right says, "Charity begins at home," they almost always forget the unspoken coda "and it usually ends there as well." The biblical idea of compassion (which literally means "feeling with") involves an innate capacity to feel what someone else feels, to experience the suffering of others empathically. We are able to do this when we are no longer "proud" but see the pain in this world with what Mary, the mother of Jesus, calls, in her song, "The Magnificat," the imagination of our hearts (Luke 1:51).

Such feelings come naturally within our own families or on behalf of our friends, but true compassion has nothing to do with caring for those that we are naturally inclined to care for. The true test of compassion is how we respond to those we are *not* naturally inclined to care for. There should be no "means test" for any response to human suffering (do they "deserve" it because they have sinned?) but rather a universal covenant to put aside blame when suffering is present and deal with human need in the moment. After all, self-inflicted suffering hurts just as much as the cruel arrows of fate.

Unfortunately, the Hebrew word for compassion is often translated into English as *mercy*, and this is a very different emotion. The connotations of mercy imply a superior in a relationship to a subordinate and are often synonymous with *pity*. Pity is bestowed, whereas compassion is engendered. Even though someone has the right to do otherwise, one "takes pity" on someone and shows mercy. It's a gift, often with strings attached, which does not remove the self from the equation. The distinction here is more than a linguistic subtlety; it betrays a fundamentally different approach to the reason why we should help others. We are not doing them a favor. We *are* the other, and the other is us.

In truth, the word *compassion* can be used to cover a multitude of political sins that show no compassion at all. There are various ways to steal from people, and sometimes we do it by explaining the benefits first. The most successful of all government programs in America is Social Security. The idea was that the present "strong" would invest in the future "weak" by contributing to a national retirement fund for everyone. We did not just "pay in" in order to "get back," like a national annuity, but rather we invested in a collective vision of social decency. Franklin Roosevelt had witnessed what the marketplace alone could provide for some retirees, even those who had worked hard all their lives, and it was a national shame. Never again would we confuse "freedom" with negligence.

The same is true of Medicare. As in any insurance program, the lucky (those who are not injured or diseased) help pay for those who are less lucky (those who are injured or diseased). This is not a sign of weakness but of true compassion. To help guarantee that the aid would be there, we decided not to gamble with the money or make such programs subject to the whims of the stock market, corrupt investment bankers, or even the bad judgment of individuals who might squander their own future. Collectively, we could be more compassionate than we had individually proved ourselves to be. We would help even those who had not been smart enough or rich enough or lucky enough to succeed in the world and thus "deserved" to retire in style. Remember, at the heart of Christian Right theology (and conservatism in general) is the belief that people "get what they deserve." There are winners and losers because that is God's moral hierarchy. Fear of losing is what motivates losers to become winners. That's what an "opportunity society" is all about. Pull yourself up by your boot straps, if you can afford the boots. If not, work harder, and then go boot shopping.

To justify the ever-widening gap between rich and poor as inevitable, the Christian Right quotes out of context one of the most misunderstood texts in the New Testament: "The poor you shall have with you always" (Matthew 26:11). If that means that poverty is inevitable, then we can all breathe a sigh of collective, guilt-ridden relief. Except that Jesus didn't mean to *excuse* poverty but to remind us that we would always have work to do! Jesus wasn't in the business of relieving guilt; his intent was to motivate people to act with compassion.

So when Republicans urge self-reliance for the poor and then fail to raise the minimum wage year after year as the cost of living rises, they are engaged in a cruel form of hypocrisy. When they cut programs that provide child care and job training to give more money to billionaires, they are revising the whole concept of compassion. By their actions, they are rewriting the text: "We will *guarantee* that the poor you shall have with you always."

Besides, let's be honest. Desperate workers without union protection are easy to manipulate and even easier to dispense with. Some people look at low wages and see a problem. Others look at low wages and see the solution. An "opportunity society" sounds wonderful, even beguiling in its egalitarianism. The rhetoric is crafted to sound compassionate, without providing any real help for the poor. In his address to the Republican National Convention, the president said, "To create more jobs in America, America must be the best place in the world to do business. To create more jobs, my plan will encourage investment and expansion by restraining federal spending, reducing regulation, and making tax relief permanent."[11]

The truth is that federal spending has not been restrained, except in social programs, but has in fact exploded into an ocean of debt. Regulations have indeed been reduced, but only for corporations that pollute, commit antitrust violations, and plunder their worker's pensions. And tax relief has indeed become permanent for the rich, especially for the wealthiest Americans, who will be able to pass along their entire estates tax-free instead of being penalized by a "death tax." After all, who could possibly be in favor of taxing people just because they died?

Besides, if the Republicans want to avoid "bearing false witness," they should stop saying that they are trying to save the family farm by eliminating the estate tax. "Let your speech be a simple yes or no," said Jesus—as opposed to a carefully crafted lie. As for this being the best place in the world to do business, it depends on whether you want to have a middle class or just an oligarchy.

Two brass rings now seem within reach of today's "compassionate conservatives": (1) control of the judiciary, which often frustrates the Right by upholding antidiscrimination laws and protecting the separation of church and state, and (2) capping damage awards in the courtroom through so-called tort reform. The first is all that stands in the way of a theocracy, and the second is all that stands in the way of corporate immunity from willful harm done to powerless consumers. Juries don't know best how much to pay the injured child. Father knows best.

In Sunday school, we all learned that compassion *is* as compassion *does*—and that "faith without works is dead." Saying that you are compassionate while promoting inequity, rewarding the already rich, and defending conspicuous consumption by sacrificing the sons and daughters of the poor is hardly compassionate. Talking about "freedom" as God's own crusade while invading and occupying another country in order to install "the most honorable form of government ever devised by man" is an exercise in pure delusion.

The rich have "opportunities" the poor will never have, just as the rich escaped the wrath of Hurricane Katrina and the poor did not. The mark of a truly religious person is humility and compassion, not the arrogance and pity of the Christian Right. God is not a partisan cheering the virtues of inner strength, discipline, and the creation of "pathways" to prosperity for other disciplined people. And freedom is not to be confused with economic survival of the fittest.

Religious freedom is the voluntary embrace of the burdens of the neighbor, not the moralizing posture of the haves lecturing the have-nots. Zell Miller, the Democratic Georgia senator who endorsed Bush in the 2004 campaign, may believe that the president has a "heart of gold" and a "spine of tempered steel," but that doesn't make it so. The "savior" of both men warned us long ago, "Beware of false prophets, who come to you in sheep's clothing but inwardly are ravenous wolves" (Matthew 7:15).

Chapter Nine

Cleansing the Temple of U.S. Health Care

> When you talk about Jesus constantly, who was a healer of the sick, but do nothing to make sure that anyone who is sick can go to see a doctor, even if she doesn't have a penny in her pocket, you are doing something immoral.

There are few issues in American life that so clearly illustrate our moral bankruptcy as the way we deliver health care. We don't. We sell disease treatment services to the insured and subsidize emergency room services for everyone else. Healing and compassion have been separated by "ability to pay," and we pay more per capita for health care than any other country. Yet we rank nineteenth in the world in infant mortality and turn our backs on a rising tide of uninsured—forty-five million and counting. This is the best health care that the temple of the marketplace can provide. Where is Jesus and his whip when we need him?

If we worship at the altar of "whatever the market will bear," we have only ourselves to blame when we look at how unbearable the situation has become. U.S. health care costs have reached $1.6 trillion a year, or 15 percent of the nation's economy. That's up from 5 percent in 1963. Other industrial nations, who may not be so loudly "Christian," devote less than 10 percent of their gross domestic product to health care. What do we have to show for our money? Some of the most unhealthy people in the civilized world. It was Martin

Luther King Jr. who noted that "there is no greater injustice than inequality in health care."[1]

One of our most common folk aphorisms is this: if you don't have your health, you don't have anything. If that's true, then what are we to make of a reputedly Christian nation that refuses to make health care a right instead of an economic privilege? All life is precious, we hear again and again, but apparently some postnatal lives are worth saving and some are not. If compassion is the defining characteristic of faithful people, then why is it that the first question we ask the sick is not "Where does it hurt?" but "Do you have insurance?"

In the early 1990s, First Lady Hillary Clinton insisted that the nation confront the health care crisis. At the time, there were thirty million uninsured, and third-party bureaucracies like HMOs were just beginning to compromise the essential doctor-patient relationship. They called themselves "health care providers," but they are, more accurately, health care *deniers*. The more health care they deny, the more money they make.

How did the Republican Party and its Christian Right base respond to the efforts of a first lady to cover more uninsured Americans? They launched an all-out assault on any reform efforts. Talk radio vilified Hillary Clinton, and preachers railed against the evils of "socialized medicine." The idea that we would submit to "government-run" health care was portrayed as the end of "you and your doctor making these important decisions together." Instead, we got a vast new medical-industrial complex where bureaucrats told doctors what they could and could not do, thus putting an end to precisely the same relationship—"you and your doctor making these important decisions together"!

The centerpiece of the propaganda campaign was a fictional couple named Harry and Louise. In a series of political "infomercials," these paid actors feigned deep concern for the future of American health care and sought to frighten us all over the prospect that the system would run out of money and we would lose the ability to chose our doctors and control our health care options.[2]

Harry and Louise were just an average suburban couple who happened to have a copy of the massive health care reform proposal on their living room coffee table. They read it to each other with the kind of disdain normally reserved for a communist manifesto. The big bad government was about to take away our medical choices and compromise our freedom to chose the best health care money can buy. Harry and Louise were there to warn us of impending doom should anyone try to fix what they insisted wasn't broken. They were white and wealthy (and probably Christian), and yet their angst was not for the "the last and the least" but for the preservation of their own privileges. They warned us to cling to a failing system because "it's all about me."

It might be wise for the church to remind people that Jesus was a healer of the sick, not the lead singer in a rock band or head of the Jerusalem Chamber of Commerce. In his first sermon, the young Jesus reads from the prophet Isaiah and then takes it upon *himself* to "give sight to the blind" (Luke 4:18). When he explains the meaning of discipleship in Matthew 25, he includes the imperative "I was sick and you took care of me" (25:36). The biblical vision of *shalom* is a covenant to seek peace by restoring wholeness to Creation and to overcome whatever alienates us from full participation in the beloved community.

Righteousness and justice are not simply abstract terms but must be promoted in relation to the human situation. If we are indeed created in the image of God and if all life is precious, then it is a violation of God's intended dignity that so many of our sisters and brothers lack access to basic health care. More important, this is not just a political issue. It's a moral issue. As theologian Walter Brueggemann and colleagues have noted, "In biblical faith, the doing of justice is the primary expectation of God."[3]

This requires that we meet human need with collective compassion, not with the creation of tax-deductible "health savings accounts." Those will do nothing to fix a system in which individuals who have more and can save more will be able to afford to buy more health care! The reign of a Sovereign God, which we love to talk about, would mean "insiders" helping to take care of more and more "outsiders." This is not just a politically correct idea; this is the Gospel.

The earliest and oldest Gospel, Mark, begins with one healing after another: a man with an unclean spirit, Simon's mother-in-law in bed with a fever, "all who were sick or possessed with demons," a leper who begged to "be made clean," a man with a withered hand (healed even on the Sabbath), a paralytic brought down through the roof of his home by determined coconspirators. A Syrophoenician woman begs Jesus to heal her daughter; a deaf man begs for help to hear and to speak; a blind man asks to have his sight restored; an epileptic boy is brought to be healed of his seizures; Bartimaeus calls out from the side of the road for healing, and Jesus responds not by handing him a form to fill out but with a simple and beautiful directive: "Call him here."

There can be no separation of concern for the spirit from care of the body. The great American tradition of nonprofit hospitals founded by religious orders and run by individuals who considered healing to be inseparable from faith are going away. Nonprofit hospitals are being gobbled up by for-profit health care corporations like Columbia/HCA. Ironically, not only does care become more expensive and more difficult to access, but now most of the religious trappings have been removed from those hospitals. It's ironic that the same Religious Right that is constantly trying to get religious symbols into the public square does not object when stockholders replace the statues of the Sisters of Mercy with the portraits of corporate raiders in the halls of healing.

In the time of Jesus, illness was thought to be caused by demonic possession. Now we know that body, mind, and spirit form a trinity of health and that even our thoughts can make us ill or make us well. Even so, there comes a time when we are asked to ease suffering and to heal disease, no matter how it came to afflict those who suffer. We can cut out tumors instead of casting out demons, but the question remains: who should get the chance to live, and who should be allowed to die?

It is very easy to spot people without health insurance these days, according to Malcolm Gladwell. They often have bad teeth because going to dentist is considered a luxury. They cover their mouths to hide toothless smiles and eat fewer and fewer fruits and vegetables. Without a winsome smile, they have trouble getting decent jobs and are put in the back somewhere, far from the public's eye. Researchers recently discovered that when asked what their first priority would be if the president established universal health coverage tomorrow, "the immediate answer was 'my teeth.'"[4]

If you dare to go channel-surfing late at night and pause to listen to most TV evangelists, you will hear a lot about getting out of debt (after first sending some of what you have left to the preacher). Debt is talked about as a scourge, a ball and chain, an albatross that hangs around the necks of the unrepentant and keeps us from the financial "victory" that God intends. Yet not a single one of these preachers will ever dare to tell the truth about what causes most personal bankruptcy in the United States: unpaid medical bills, according to a Harvard study.[5] Half the uninsured in America owe money to hospitals, and one-third are being pursued by collection agencies. Without insurance, people get sick more often and lose their jobs at a higher rate than the insured. Lack of access to regular preventive health care is a downward spiral just like violence, and an ounce of prevention really is worth a pound of cure.

Jesus may have healed people constantly, and Luke was a physician, but the Christian Right has been a crucial element in the resistance to every attempt (six in the past century) to introduce some kind of universal health care system in America. The health care system we accept is so dysfunctional and unjust that we spend more and get less than most other countries. We have fewer doctors, make fewer appointments, and get admitted to the hospital less frequently than those in other Western nations. We don't like our health care system, have a lower life expectancy, and have disgraceful rates of infant mortality and immunization. Our doctors perform more expensive procedures while general practice languishes. The fastest-growing area of medicine is cosmetic plastic surgery. Consider the morality of a nip and a tuck when some of God's children are pulling out their own teeth.

To understand why we are among the few remaining industrialized nations that do not provide basic health care to all its citizens, you must acknowledge what Malcolm Gladwell calls the "moral-hazard myth."[6] *Moral hazard* is a term that economists use to describe the fact that "insurance can change the behavior of the person being insured. If your office gives you and your co-workers all the free Pepsi you want—if your employer, in effect, offers universal Pepsi insurance—you'll drink more Pepsi than you would have otherwise." Hence the pervasive belief that insurance can have "the paradoxical effect of producing risky and wasteful behavior."

This is why insurance companies require us to make a $20 co-payment when we visit the doctor. It's not just an attempt to get us to pick up a larger share of our health care costs, Gladwell writes. "It is an attempt to make your use of the health-care system more efficient." It will reduce "moral hazard: you'll no longer grab one of those free Pepsis when you aren't really thirsty."[7]

Those who accept the moral hazard theory of insurance are not alarmed by forty-five million uninsured Americans. The uninsured spend, on average, $934 a year on medical care. The insured, on the other hand, spend $2,347 per year. One could argue, therefore, that the uninsured are the truly efficient consumers of health care.

This is true, Gladwell argues, only if you accept the argument that people consume health care in the same way they consume other goods and services. They do not. We go to the doctor reluctantly, because we are sick. "Moral hazard is overblown," says Princeton economist Uwe Reinhardt. Rich people who have great private insurance don't check into the hospital because it's free. "Do people really like to go to the doctor? Do they check into the hospital instead of playing golf?"

As it turns out, when people are asked to pay more for their own care, they get less care, and the care they get is of poorer quality. Studies have shown that people opt out of routine checkups and preventive care most often to save money. And that ends up costing everyone in the long run.

This may be what all those other countries have figured out, but the Bush administration proposes health savings accounts because it accepts the moral hazard myth. In fact, the Bushies believe that Americans have too much health insurance, and this leads to over-consumption and waste. They even believe, as indicated by the 2004 Economic Report of the President, that a large number of Americans "remain uninsured as a matter of choice."

This view of America as a place where the uninsured are the most efficient consumers of health care and the insured are waste-ful is as disconnected from reality as FEMA's response to recent nat-ural disasters and the president's progress reports on the war. We are increasingly living in parallel universes where the rich seem obliv-ious to the very existence of the poor and then blithely unrespon-sive to a situation that must, after all, be of their own making.

This disconnect was never more poignantly expressed than when the president's mother looked at the hurricane evacuees in the Hous-ton Astrodome and said, "What I'm hearing, which is sort of scary, is that they all want to stay in Texas. Everyone is so overwhelmed by the hospitality. And so many of the people in the arena here, you know, were underprivileged anyway, so this—this is working very well for them."[8]

So let's see if we understand this brave new world. Those who study the health care crisis in America have determined that there is too little of it, while the president's men and women look at the same situation and determine that there is too much. The former group of scholars, using the kind of empirical research that is as eas-ily dismissed by the Right as the research on global warming (or evolution for that matter), makes it clear that *poverty* is to blame. In the government's own economic report, which addresses people who are offered insurance but "decline the coverage" as a "matter of choice," the word *poverty* is never used. It may not have occurred to the president that they "decline" it because they can't afford it.

Our way of delivering health care is personal and private, while the rest of the world has adopted a model of coverage known as "social insurance." The elderly man with heart problems doesn't pay more because he is sick. Rather, the young healthy man pays more in premiums now so that someday the system will subsidize his health care when he is old and needs more expensive care. In other words, strange as this may sound in such a "devout" nation, the strong help to bear the infirmities of the weak.

America is one of the last places left on earth where every citizen, until the day he or she dies, is exposed to the risk of personal bankruptcy because of illness or disease. It does not matter how industrious we are, how carefully we save and invest, or how moral we are in our personal and family life. We are all just one long hospital stay away from losing everything. That possibility, looming in the back of everyone's mind, is the cause of constant anxiety. As the evidence mounts that our present system is broken beyond the point of repair, politicians who babble about Jesus constantly pass laws that move us in the opposite direction. Health savings accounts do not move us toward universal health care. They are the antithesis of universal health care.

It is also deeply ironic that the same crowd that hates Darwin should be so zealously wedded to a governing philosophy that is so Darwinian. Survival of the fittest is obvious in nature, but shouldn't human beings elevate themselves to a higher order? We forget that in the clamor of opinions about health care, real human beings suffer and die because the inequities are so vast, and the gap grows wider every day.

How can we speak of stewardship and community and compassion and allow a broken health care system to move in a direction that is the antithesis of each of those religious ideas? If we are indeed our brother's and sister's keepers, and if love is all there is in this beautiful, terrible, wonderful world, then how can we make access to health care a test of wealth? We can do this only if we believe that wealth is sign of God's favor and poverty is a form of God's disfavor. We can only do this because in our greed and stupidity we are fundamentally separated from each other, and we have accepted the unacceptable with the help of bad theology.

To all those who thought they knew the mind of God on the merits of wealth and poverty, Jesus told the story of Lazarus and the rich man. Dressed in purple and fine linen and "feasting sumptuously every day," the rich man has found a way to ignore and step over a poor beggar who lies just outside his gate and might as well be invisible. They both die, and the poor man is carried away by angels to be with Abraham. The rich man is tormented in Hades.

Looking up and seeing Abraham with Lazarus by his side, the rich man begs for mercy, asking only to have Lazarus dip the tip of his finger in water and cool off his tongue. But Abraham says, "Child, remember that during your lifetime you received your good things and Lazarus in like manner evil things; but now he is comforted here, and you are in agony. Besides all this, between you and us a great chasm has been fixed, so that those who might want to pass from here to you cannot do so, and no one can cross from there to us" (Luke 16:25–26).

That "great chasm" describes the two worlds in which the rich and poor live. Hurricane Katrina came roaring across that chasm and literally flushed the poor of New Orleans out of hiding and into the national consciousness. They had been lying outside the national gate while the rest of us were feasting inside. We might have been able to heal the sores of Lazarus, instead of having them licked by dogs, if only we had noticed him and taken him to see a doctor sooner.

Did the rich man not know that the beggar was hungry? Do the rest of us not know that countless children go to bed hungry in this country every night? What's more, that we waste enough food every day to feed a small country? Perhaps, as we stand over our granite countertops in our suburban castles and scrape enough food into the garbage disposal every day to feed another family, we might actually hear the words of Jesus as something other than comfort or financial advice.

Princeton's Cornel West put it best: "What we saw unfold in the days after the hurricane was the most naked manifestation of conservative social policy toward the poor, where the message for decades has been, 'You are on your own.' . . . People said: 'It looks like something out of the Third World.' Well, New Orleans was Third World long before the hurricane."[9]

If the way the strong treat the weak is the ultimate ethical test, we have failed miserably when it comes to health care. The market can deliver many nonessential items without being immoral. But it cannot be allowed to deliver "being" and "nonbeing" without collapsing upon itself. Medical care is not a choice like other choices because the consequences of others choices are not fatal. We will pay whatever we have to pay or go as deeply into debt as we must in order to save ourselves or those we love. Many things we can do without, but not health care. It should be one of those things that *we all do for each other*. It would be very "pro-life."

That is, if we still believe that "moral issues" are also "social justice" issues, then we must move toward a national health care system for all Americans. This could be done with just a portion of the cost of the recent tax cuts for the rich. Four years ago, we passed a $1.6 trillion tax cut. Had that tax cut been a mere $1 trillion (still the largest in history), we could have used the $600 billion to fund a comprehensive health insurance program for a decade.

"One Nation Under God"—what does that really mean? A professor of economics at Princeton University, Uwe Reinhart, says that all our budget decisions are really moral decisions. We might as well have sent a memo to God, he said, which goes something like this: "Dear God, We had to decide between health insurance and a tax cut, and we took all the money as a tax cut. We hope this pleases you. Signed, A Grateful Nation."[10]

Chapter Ten

Christian Fascism and
the War on Reason

When you put judges on the bench who are racist and will set
women back a hundred years, and when you surround yourself with preachers who say gays ought to be killed, you are
dong something immoral.

One of the most controversial columns that I have ever written for
the *Oklahoma Gazette* was titled "Using the F-Word." It was an attempt to get readers to understand that fascism is not solely reserved
for goose-stepping, jackbooted Nazis. There is a Christian fascism on
the rise in America, and the signs are unmistakable. We don't like to
admit it, so we chase this ugly thought from our minds, feigning disgust at the word. After all, we defeated fascism. Surely we would never
allow it to rise in our country, would we?

Scholars will argue over the precise definition of fascism, but Mussolini knew the essence of it: the merger of corporate and government
power. Political scientist Lawrence Britt recently published a concise
list of the fourteen characteristics of fascism, and it should have sent
a chill down the spine of everyone who is still reading. He studied the
regimes of Hitler, Mussolini, Franco, Suharto, and Pinochet and
found that they all had these things in common: (1) powerful and
continuing nationalism, (2) disdain for the recognition of human
rights, (3) identification of enemies and scapegoats as a unifying cause,

(4) supremacy of the military, (5) rampant sexism, (6) controlled mass media, (7) obsession with national security, (8) religion and government intertwined, (9) protection of corporate power, (10) suppression of labor power, (11) disdain for intellectuals and the arts, (12) obsession with crime and punishment, (13) rampant cronyism and corruption, and (14) fraudulent elections.[1]

Which of these characteristics is not obvious and ascendant in America today? The disturbing but vital truth is that they *all* are, and the Christian Right has energized the entire agenda with the reputed blessings of a Republican God. Consider them one by one, and ask yourself whether the handwriting is not on the wall, in red, white, and born-again blue?

A gaudy, knee-jerk patriotism is back, flags are everywhere, and they are huge. People look the other way when we torture prisoners, convinced that an ill-defined threat justifies the suspension of our own legal standards. Talk radio fills the air with hatred against "enemies," which is anyone who disagrees with the Right. Military spending soars, social spending dwindles, and the cult of soldier worship is a national pastime. According to its own internal study, the Air Force Academy admitted that 12 percent of its female cadets reported being raped in 2003, and in many institutions, gays are the new scapegoat. A corporate media rails against a nonexistent "liberal media bias" while engaging in rampant right-wing propaganda. A color-coded system of "threat levels" keeps the civilian population continually fearful. The government wears Christianity on its sleeve while ignoring the basic teachings of Jesus.

Big business supplies government leaders in a revolving door of mutual favors. Labor unions are vilified, and so-called right-to-work legislation weakens them under the guise of attracting new industry. Intellectual acumen is belittled as a form of elitism, and artists are portrayed as dangerous, unpatriotic, and subversive. Personal friends are rewarded with government jobs, and incompetence is overlooked, even rewarded, so long as loyalty is unwavering. The election process gradually disintegrates into confusion, allegations of fraud, and partisan manipulation to suppress opposing voter turnout or disqualify votes that threaten the status quo.

Let it not be said, however, that no one is trying to warn us. One of the most eloquent prophets in the land once trained to be a Baptist minister but became a journalist instead. Bill Moyers has been sounding warnings about the Christian Right for years and has lived to see his worst fears come true (and his PBS program *Now* spied on for evidence of liberal bias). When Union Seminary in New York awarded its highest honor, the Union Medal, to Bill and Judith Moyers, it was for his work to promote "faith and reason in America." The irony, of course, is that faith and reason have a long history of bitter conflict and are now so separated by today's fundamentalists that they are considered mortal enemies. It's a lie, of course, because faith and reason need one another and are not mutually exclusive. The danger now comes not from liberals who think about their faith and respect science but from religious fanatics who run the country and are close to realizing their version of heaven on earth: an American theocracy.

In a stirring address at Union Seminary, Moyers sounded a deep, clear, and prophetic warning about the takeover of the Republican Party by the Christian Right and their plans to seize control of the last remaining obstacle to a theocracy: the judiciary.[2] If they can appoint judges who will enforce "biblical law" and turn away from secular reason and logic as the indispensable tools of a free and pluralistic society, the last remaining obstacle to Christian fascism will be removed.

The culture wars are rooted in biblical literalism and the desire by some Christians to have an absolute standard of moral conduct that is just as infallible as the Bible from which it comes. Oddly enough, biblical literalism is itself an artificial imposition on the poets and mythmakers who wrote the literature, which was ultimately gathered up, edited, and deemed "sacred." It is always wise to remember, as one of my seminary professors pointed out, that not a single person whose words ultimately became part of the Bible had any idea that he or she was writing a part of the Bible. What's more, none of them wrote in English, meaning that the various translations (and mistranslations) that we now possess cannot possibly be the *literal* Word of God.

So while we are fond of saying, "The Bible *says* this and the Bible *says* that," the truth is that "the Bible *said* this or that." Not a single word of the Bible is addressed to a single one of us. We "overhear" it[3] and must determine how to bring forward a fresh take that is true to the spirit of the text without pretending that we live in the first century. That means we must "interpret" the Bible, and that is fraught with danger. The only thing more dangerous is *not* interpreting it— carefully, critically, honestly.

Asking intelligent human beings to accept the Bible at face value is to invite the best and the brightest among us to either leave the church or pretend to believe things we know are not true. Fundamentalists have always suspected that the tools of higher criticism poke holes in the dyke, which invariably results in the breaking of the dam of faith. But what does it mean to say the Bible is "inspired"? As the words lie on the page? As only certain church leaders interpret them? As only certain faith communities interpret them?

"Theologians" as gifted as Pat Robertson and indicted senator Tom DeLay now insist that the only true approach to the Bible is uncritical obedience and mindless acceptance. Never mind that the Bible contains numerous demonstrable errors if one reads literally: Ezekiel makes predictions about the destruction of Tyre by Nebuchadrezzar and Babylon's conquest of Egypt that are simply wrong. Technically speaking, Jesus is not in the grave "three days and three nights," and Jesus once quotes a scriptural verse that does not exist (John 7:38). If God is omnipotent, why does the Bible say he needs rest or needs to walk anywhere, as he does in the Garden of Eden?

Biblical infallibility has turned the Bible into what Protestants would call a "paper pope" and requires intelligent men and women to abandon their own critical thinking skills. It is our human need for absolute certainty that asks of the Bible what it cannot deliver, and it is sinful for us not to want to think, to reason, and to love the Lord our God will all our heart, soul, and *mind*.

What's more, reading the Bible literally makes belief in a loving God impossible. If God did indeed order the slaughter of other human beings, including women and children, as Scripture reports, then God is little more than a cruel and capricious partisan. If God is merely an extension of our own prejudices, one who defends his friends and smites his enemies, then what good does it do us to call on God's name? Yet this is exactly the kind of God the Christian Right seems drawn to.

It needs a macho God to justify its own blood-soaked agenda. No wonder fundamentalists fear a literary or critical study of the Bible. Such a study would disassemble their case for divine hatred. No wonder they gravitate toward the primitive Storm God often portrayed in the Old Testament and away from the Loving and Forgiving Father of the New Testament. The New Covenant, whose only commandment is that we love our neighbor as ourselves, would undermine their case for privilege, hierarchy, and the fear of divine wrath.

The members of the Christian Right are always telling us what's on God's mind, but what they are really telling us is what's on *their* minds. They have the right to interpret the Bible in any way they choose, of course, but they do not have the right to tell the rest of us what it means to be a Christian. They can say that 9/11 and Hurricane Katrina were God's punishment for the wicked, but they cannot try to silence the rest of us who find such assertions both repugnant and dangerous. They can peddle a theology of hatred, condemnation, and cruelty if they wish, but they cannot question the patriotism or the faith of those who believe that the Gospel is not infinitely malleable and that anything goes if you are wearing a clerical robe or a lapel flag pin.

Bill Moyers describes the near total takeover of the Christian Right by warning us that "freedom" is a relative term for fundamentalists. And reason applies only if the reasoning leads to the right answer; otherwise it is an instrument of the Devil.

Listen to their preachers, evangelists, and homegrown ayatollahs: Their viral intolerance—their loathing of other people's beliefs, of America's secular and liberal values, of an independent press, of the courts, of reason, science, and the search for objective knowledge—has become an unprecedented sectarian crusade for state power. They use the language of faith to demonize political opponents, mislead and misinform voters, censor writers and artists, ostracize dissenters, and marginalize the poor. These are the foot soldiers in a political holy war financed by wealthy economic interests and guided by savvy partisan operatives who know that couching political ambition in religious rhetoric can ignite the passion of followers as ferociously as when Constantine painted the Sign of Christ (the "Christograph") on the shields of his soldiers and on the banner of his legions and routed his rivals in Rome. Never mind that the Emperor himself was never baptized into the faith; it served him well enough to make the God worshiped by Christians his most important ally and turn the Sign of Christ into the one imperial symbol most widely recognized and feared from east to west.[4]

Who are these loyal foot soldiers? They are megachurch pastors like Rod Parsley, whose $40 million-a-year ministry in Columbus, Ohio, is part of what's called the Ohio Restoration Project, training thousands of what he calls "patriot pastors." Their charge will not be to follow Jesus by helping the poor but to become crusaders for Christ, energized by the certain knowledge that we are approaching the End Times. The next election will be an apocalyptic battle for the soul of the nation, and God's Own Party must win, or God loses. The agenda is based on demonizing the other, whom he calls "the very hordes of hell in our society," and by appeals to sexual deviancy and fear. In between railing against the "pagan left" and the gay rights movement as the last sign of our moral collapse, Parsley pauses to thank Jesus. As venom spews out one side of his mouth, all "glory, laud, and honor" are given to the name of the Prince of Peace out the other. While judging, condemning, and verbally crucifying the enemies of civilization, prayers are offered in the name of a radical teacher of alternative wisdom executed by the religious establishment of his day for being a threat to moral order and decency. Pure hatred, followed by "Thank you, Jesus!"

If this doesn't seem to make any sense, that's because reason itself is often considered the enemy of the Christian Right. The antics of the Kansas Board of Education and countless other defenders of compulsory theism in public schools remind us that science is still the enemy of fundamentalists everywhere. Intelligent design, which is simply the latest euphemism for creationism, proves that the Scopes Monkey Trial may have been decided but is being infinitely appealed. Often local school boards are taken by surprise when "stealth candidates" keep their radical religious views a secret during the campaign. After they are seated, and often quite to the surprise of parents and administrators, they introduce resolutions to place "disclaimers" in biology textbooks warning students that evolution is "just a theory."

The example they set and the reasoning they employ would make it impossible for them to pass the classes they are regulating! Of course evolution is a theory, and a scientific one at that. Almost every scientist in the world believes it, but anyone is free not to. What none of us are free to do is lie to our children and tell them that intelligent design is a *scientific* theory. It is a religious belief, based on a literal interpretation of Genesis. It can and should be taught as a religious belief, along with all the other Creation myths. For one thing, it would be a perfect opportunity to show students that there are two very different accounts of Creation in Genesis, only one of which conflicts with the theory of evolution.

What is disingenuous and dangerous is for adults to teach by example that one can believe something first and then "fix the intelligence around it," to quote the Downing Street Memo.[5] For educators to manipulate the definition of science is to destroy the very idea of science, which is careful observation, collection and analysis of data, and findings drawn from evidence and inference, not from a priori assumptions.

The problem is that we have the first-ever Christian fundamentalist in the White House, and his disdain for science, reason, and objective knowledge is clear. He scoffs at evidence of global warming, bows to political pressure on stem cell research, and exhibits a kind of arrogant impatience with careful, reasoned discourse. There is a saying that sums up the president's attitude toward hard science: "Don't confuse me with the facts."

But the facts are exactly what have been missing as the Christian Right has risen to power. The facts do indeed "confuse" people because they are the only check against a completely choreographed, media-controlled reality. The political speeches, the sound bites, the flags, the martial music—they all work their magic on average voters. But those dedicated to the life of the mind are much harder to control. Scientists, lawyers, judges, journalists, and college professors are stubbornly wedded to critical thinking, the use of evidence, and the redeeming value of cogent reasoning. While teachers and professors are often vilified for being "secular humanists" by people who have never set foot in a classroom, it is now the judiciary that draws the most fire from the Christian Right. In the ever-shifting list of enemies of the Right, the judges are the new target, the "vermin in black robes," as one radio talk show host called them.[6]

Because they serve life appointments and have made a career out of following and evaluating arguments based on evidence, they are less prone to visceral or emotional decisions. That is, they are more difficult to control with emotional appeals and religious propaganda. They infuriate the Christian Right precisely because they often hand down rulings that frustrate the dream of a theocracy, ruling in favor of preserving civil liberties and the rights of minorities, religious or otherwise. For this reason, the Christian Right has declared a "holy war on the judiciary."

The fundamentalists have organized so-called Justice Sundays in large megachurches and take turns blasting what is now a conservative Supreme Court for being what James Dobson calls an "oligarchy." Indicted House Majority Leader Tom DeLay of Texas claims that the Supreme Court has usurped the power of Congress to make laws and is guilty of "judicial supremacy and autocracy."[7] He once refused to stand trial in a courtroom because the judge was a Democrat.

The president of the Catholic League for Religious and Civil Rights, William Donohue, said the high court is so out of control that it needs a constitutional amendment to say that "unless a judicial vote is unanimous, you cannot overturn a law created by Congress." He also went on to say, "I'm going to try to do my job to intimidate the Senate Judiciary Committee so they do their job more carefully." When asked by a reporter if he meant to use the word *intimidate*, he answered, "Absolutely."[8]

The organizer of one Justice Sunday was Tony Perkins, president of the Family Research Council. He said the high court had legalized the killing of unborn children and "homosexual sodomy." Never mind that most Americans see these issues in a much more nuanced way, with a plurality of the public now supporting either civil union or marriage for gay and lesbian couples, or that on abortion rights there is an even stronger consensus that this is "settled law," with 60 percent of Americans supporting *Roe* v. *Wade*. Sixty-five percent also say they want a new Supreme Court justice who will uphold a woman's right to choose, compared to only 29 percent who want a justice to help overturn it.

When John Roberts was confirmed as Chief Justice of the United States, the Christian Right won a major victory through the nomination of what many consider the perfect stealth candidate. Saying only enough to be confirmed, Judge Roberts brings rock-solid conservative credentials to a court that continues to move to the right. The Bush administration refused to release documents that might have shed light on his judicial philosophy, continuing a pattern of secrecy that has been its hallmark. In particular, senators asked for documents detailing Roberts's work on sixteen critical cases during his time as principal deputy to Solicitor Ken Starr in the George H. W. Bush administration.

Those cases involved efforts to restrict key rights and freedoms in the courts and would give the judiciary committee crucial information on Roberts's views on voting rights, affirmative action, privacy and reproductive choice, school desegregation, the separation of church and state, environmental protection, and discrimination in federally funded education programs against women, minorities, people with disabilities, and other Americans. The memos were blocked, and the American people now have a Chief Justice who may serve for three decades or more and about whom they know very little.

With the aborted nomination of Harriet Miers, the president's personal lawyer, Bush again demonstrated that he prefers loyalty to qualifications. With the subsequent nomination and confirmation of Samuel Alito, he also proved that the Christian Right is calling the shots. No one doubted Alito's qualifications, but everyone agrees that he will move the court radically to the right.

When the president ran for office in 2000, he made promises about seeking consensus candidates and changing the politically charged, adversarial ways of Washington. Then he nominated the most ideologically extreme candidates ever put forth by an American president. When Democrats fought those nominations, Republican leaders in Congress threatened to end the Senate's right to filibuster, employing the so-called nuclear option. Cloaked in a kind of entitlement secrecy and brought forward with the rhetoric of religious certainty (every Bush nominee will "do a great job and make us all proud," no matter how inept the person turns out to be), a slate of judges so extreme was put forward that the Democrats were made to look like obstructionists for blocking them.

This way of doing things is perfectly congruent with a "win at all costs" mentality and the self-righteous fervor of those who are on a crusade to "save us" from the tyranny of whatever stands in God's way. President Bush promised to nominate judges "exceptional for their humanity." Here are just a few quotations that are part of the public record from the mouths of the "exceptional" human beings that Bush nominated to serve as federal judges:

William Pryor called *Roe* versus *Wade* an "abomination." Charles Pickering called a cross-burning incident a "drunken prank." Jay Bybee advised the president that he could ignore laws forbidding torture. Carolyn Kuhl ruled that a woman's right to privacy was not violated by the doctor who invited a drug salesman to sit in on her breast exam. Jeffrey Sutton said the Americans with Disabilities Act "is not needed." Janice Rodger Brown accused senior citizens on Social Security of "cannibalizing" their grandchildren's future. William Myers compared the government's role in protecting public lands to King George's "tyrannical" rule over the American colonies. Perhaps the most conservative nominee, California Justice Janice R. Brown, called Social Security part of the government's "socialist revolution."[9]

Republicans also continue to peddle the myth that Democrats have blocked an unreasonable number of Republican nominees and created a "judicial emergency."

> In reality, Bush has had more judicial nominees approved than in the first terms of Presidents Clinton and Reagan and the administration of his father. Of the 214 nominees sent to the Senate for a vote during his first term, Democrats blocked only ten, using the filibuster. As such, 95 percent of Bush's nominees have been approved. By contrast, from 1995 to 2000, while Republican Senator Orrin Hatch was chairman of the Judiciary Committee, the Senate blocked 35 percent of Clinton's circuit court nominees.[10]

Strict father theology also translates into a patriarchal judicial philosophy. J. Leon Homes, Bush judicial nominee for the Eastern District of Arkansas, argued that a wife should "subordinate herself to her husband." Claude Allen, the president's newly appointed chief domestic policy adviser, once criticized an elected official because of his "ties with queers." These are not exceptional human beings, any more than Mike Brown was an exceptional choice to head the Federal Emergency Management Agency before we learned that he was unqualified and clueless or that John Bolton should be our UN ambassador when he has a reputation for terrorizing subordinates and doesn't believe in the United Nations. He said once, "There's no such thing as the United Nations. If the U.N. secretary building in New York lost 10 stories, it wouldn't make a bit of difference."[11]

To understand the steady march of Christian fascism, all Americans, regardless of their religious beliefs, must understand the fundamentalist mind-set and the power of judges to change the American landscape for generations. For the true believer, there are no gray areas. There is no such thing as "situation ethics." The concepts of "plurality" and "multiculturalism" are the sworn enemies of the theocracy they envision and must be defeated by any means. The heart and soul of the biblical literalist are marked by an aversion to reason and a hostility toward science. If any other point of view is valid, they believe, then my point of view must be compromised. If other people have some claim on that mysterious and dangerous thing called truth, then I must not have the market cornered. If I don't have the market cornered, my world collapses, and with it all the defenses I have marshaled to protect myself from doubt and despair. There is, in the end, no one on earth quite as dangerous as a fundamentalist trying desperately to avoid dealing with life as it really is, with people as they really are, or with a God whose love and grace are beyond comprehension.

Televangelist Jimmy Swaggart said in a sermon that he opposed gay marriage because "I've never seen a man in my life I wanted to marry. . . . And I'm going to be blunt and plain: If one ever looks at me like that, I'm going to kill him and tell God he died."[12] His Baton Rouge congregation laughed and applauded. He later apologized, saying that he has jokingly used the expression "killing someone and telling God he died" thousands of times about all sorts of people. He said the expression is figurative and not meant to harm.

We don't buy it, Mr. Swaggart. The harm is already done, and the word is already out. Violence in the name of God is becoming a national habit. Saying outrageous things that appeal to the worst human instincts and then apologizing after the fact is also becoming a standard rhetorical strategy of the Christian Right. The deed gets done, and then the offender can take credit for being contrite. The effect is to numb the national conscience by gradually making the outrageous seem commonplace.

More and more we are asked to obsess over sexual immorality and ignore the immorality of war, the neglect of the poor, and the sin of environmental degradation. Let us not forget that the whole nation was whipped into a righteous frenzy over an exposed breast at the 2004 Super Bowl halftime show. Now a preacher with a penchant for prostitutes can advocate killing someone on television and church folk find it funny.

The game is up, and the rest of us had better get off the sidelines. The forces that threaten the soul of this nation and the church depend on the inertia of good people everywhere and our reluctance to confront the forces that have hijacked the American dream and religious liberty. The Right needs us to be too busy to notice, too burdened with private ambition to get involved, too intimidated by religious rhetoric to challenge the perversion of religious principles. We have surrendered power to men who will take whatever we will give them and return none of it to us out of the goodness of their hearts. The call to revolution is now unmistakably upon us. If we do not act now, when? If not against this threat, against which greater one?

The sad truth is that the silence of the mainline churches has made the Christian Right grow even bolder. We talk about a "fearless love," but we have sentimentalized it into a Hallmark card. The Jesus who cleansed the Temple and called religious hypocrites a "brood of vipers" has devolved from a radically disturbing presence into a domesticated icon, "meek and mild, gentle as a child." Too many of us want to "keep the peace" instead of waging peace. Like the Church Lady from the old *Saturday Night Live* skit, we are a cartoon of discipleship, full of gossip, preoccupied with trivia, and dedicated to nothing that might turn our religious shortcuts into "the long and winding road" that leads to peace.

When Bill Moyers came to the end of his speech at Union Seminary, he invoked the name of Reinhold Niebuhr, perhaps the most important and most forgotten theologian of the twentieth century. In the 1940s, under the dark clouds of war, Niebuhr, who taught at Union, tried to remind his students that the idea of original sin may be troublesome for the modern mind, but it is most fully apparent when fallible human beings play God. We are not an "innocent nation," as we were fond of thinking, even before 9/11. As to our right to invade Iraq because God calls us to "spread freedom and democracy," Niebuhr wrote, "A democracy cannot of course engage in an explicit preventative war," and he lamented the "inability to comprehend the depth of evil to which individuals and communities may sink, particularly when they try to play the role of God to history." In a line that is pure prophecy, Niebuhr wrote, "Nations, as individuals, who are completely innocent in their own esteem, are insufferable in their human contacts."[13]

Original sin may not be a popular idea, but Niebuhr warned us not to forget the atrocities we have committed, even as we have fought back against the atrocities of others. What's more, self-delusion is the essence of sin, and religion is both a source of wisdom and light and a source of danger in political life, "precisely because it introduces absolutes into the realm of relative values." Its role ought to be to make us humble, not to justify our arrogance. "The worst corruption," he warned us, "is a corrupt religion."

Does this mean we ought to withdraw from the world and consider political engagement to be futile and corrupting? To decide this is to forfeit power to those who are always tempted to claim God "too simply as the sanctifier of whatever we most fervently desire." In 1952, in a work called "The Irony of American History," Niebuhr penned a warning that sounds as if it were written yesterday: "If we should perish, the ruthlessness of the foe would be only the secondary cause of the disaster. The primary cause would be that the strength of a giant nation was directed by eyes too blind to see all the hazards of the struggle; and the blindness would be induced not by some accident of nature or history but by hatred and vainglory."

We have no choice but to fight for the things we believe in through the political process because, as Niebuhr put it, "Man's capacity for justice makes democracy possible; but man's inclination to injustice makes democracy necessary." He knew that America has always had a tendency toward self-righteous delusions of innocence and infallibility. "From the earliest days of its history to the present moment, there is a deep layer of messianic consciousness in the mind of America. We never dreamed that we would have as much political power as we possess today; nor for that matter did we anticipate that the most powerful nation on earth would suffer such an ironic refutation of its dreams of mastering history."

We must turn our attention now to the enormous task that lies before us. If every generation is charged to recognize what is required of it and then carry out that obligation, our charge is to resist Christian fascism and the war against reason. It will not be easy, but then nothing worthwhile is ever easy. It will require that we admit to being part of the problem by virtue of our timidity and acquiescence. It will require that we ask more of ourselves than the intellectual sport of being a mad prophet decrying the hypocrisies of our time—especially when we don't even bother to vote. It will demand more of us than bumper stickers, bad Bush jokes, and the faux angst of "yeah, it's awful, but what can one person do?"

For starters, you don't have to be a person of religious faith to join the resistance. We need the help of all thoughtful people of goodwill and good conscience—even if you gave up on the church a long time ago. If you still know that justice requires sacrifice and that compassion is not a form of weakness, the knock of history has now come to your door. Get up and answer it.

We need people who know that a moral economy is as important as a moral individual and that discrimination of any kind is wrong, whether you are a believer, an atheist, or an agnostic. We need the spirit of another age to return, when another tragic war split the nation: "Won't you please come to Chicago, or else join the other side," sang Crosby, Stills, Nash, and Young in 1970. "We can change the world. Rearrange the world. It's dying—if you believe in justice. It's dying—and if you believe in freedom. It's dying. . . ."[14]

Time to put down the remote, turn the page, and lace up your boots.

Part Three

A Call to Nonviolent Resistance

How to Save the Country and the Church

We must be the change we wish to see in the world.
—Mahatma Gandhi

I'm tired of people thinking that because I'm a Christian, I must be a supporter of President Bush, or that because I favor civil rights and gay rights, I must not be a person of faith. I'm tired of people saying that I can't support the troops but oppose the war.

I heard that when I was your age, when the Vietnam war was raging. We knew that that war was wrong, and you know that this war is wrong—the only question is how many people are going to die before these make-believe Christians are removed from power.

This country is bankrupt. The war is morally bankrupt. The claim of this administration to be Christian is bankrupt. And the only people who can turn things around are people like you—people who are just beginning to wake up to what is

happening to them. It's your country to take back. It's your
faith to take back. It's your future to take back.

Resistance Causes Change

There is a deep and deadly fiction in the land that if enough of us get
mad enough, the walls of Christian fascism will tumble down. If
enough of us get together on a regular basis with like-minded people
and complain bitterly about the sad state of world affairs, the sad state
of world affairs will change. If we visit enough anti-Bush Web sites or
post enough clever rants on our blogs or send enough money to our
favorite liberal causes, the iron fist of political power and religious bigotry will begin to loosen and Isaiah's vision of the peaceable kingdom
will sweep over Washington, D.C. "The wolf shall lie down with the
lamb, the leopard shall lie down with the kid, the calf and the lion
and the fatling, and a little child shall lead them" (Isaiah 11:6).

Most of my friends seem to think that this will happen after coffee or, to be more specific, after a "grande iced half-caf triple-mocha
latte macchiato." It will happen after we organize and attend the perfect peace and justice seminar sponsored by members of the university philosophy club. It will happen when enough people read enough
wisdom literature, light enough candles, and learn to meditate. It will
happen, in other words, when enlightenment renders revolution unnecessary. Therefore, it will *not* happen.

You may find such sentiments surprising from a preacher. Do I
not live by hope? Do I not encourage individual human transformation every Sunday? Do I not believe the world can be changed
one life at a time? Of course I do.

But I also know that there are two kinds of time in which human
beings live: *organic* time, when things unfold naturally and history
moves us toward progress and peace, and *critical* time, when the fate
of the future hangs in the balance and human beings must seize history and turn it in another direction. In critical time, we forfeit the
luxury of indecision and apathy. World events force us to be mindful
and to act and to participate in the political process. Critical time

puts critical choices before us and then judges inaction or mindless acquiescence in the harsh light of complicity. *These are critical times*.

Ironically, the Christian Right also decided long ago that we live in critical times and has persuaded millions that the battle is between God and the godless. But the zealots' vision for America is strikingly different from the biblical vision of *shalom*. Meanwhile, the deafening silence from the rest of the church and the shameful number of people who don't even bother to vote have effectively ceded power to people who think nothing of defining true religion, true patriotism, and true morality for the rest of us.

Make no mistake—they will *not* be appeased by thoughtful arguments or appeals to compassion and equality. They must be *opposed*, as Bill Moyers put it, "with a stubbornness to match their own. . . . Christian realism requires us to see the world as it is, without illusions, and then take it on."[1]

In these critical times, intellectual angst is not enough, and thinking the right thoughts is no substitute for taking the right action. What we are up against is power, money, and religious fanaticism all wrapped up together. Such an entrenched machine depends for its existence on a kind of mindless detachment of the masses, what George Orwell in *1984* called "the proles," the stupid, disengaged, struggling multitudes who pass their time gambling and dreaming of instant wealth to dull the pain of poverty and powerlessness.

To change things, we will have to step out of the world of private ambition and into the world of *collective resistance*. There are very concrete, very specific, very powerful things that we can do to take back the country and the church, but only if we turn our anger into something positive and proactive. Anger burns us up and is often selfish in nature, but *righteous indignation* channels anger on behalf of others and sustains the soul in the struggle.

The word *indignation* derives from the same Latin root that gives us *indignity*—the opposite of dignity. Indignation is aroused not in response to injury to oneself but in response to a fundamental injustice that denies dignity to others. As the Christian Right brings back an angry God, the rest of us might want to consider bringing back an indignant God, a God who is burned up over our injustices toward one another.

Descartes' maxim was not, after all, "I think, therefore I have acted." Pure cognition cannot save the world. Sometimes intelligent people need to take to the streets because although knowledge is important, it is not redemptive. Tell a friend to quit smoking because it will kill her, and she will invariably say, "I know." Tell a kid to quit using drugs because it can steal his future, and the kid will say, "I know." Tell a cheating husband to consider whether the affair is worth losing his family, his career, and his reputation, and he will almost always say, "Of course not." So obviously, *knowing* is not enough.

The truth is that the longest trip a human being will ever take is the journey from the head to the heart. The road to hell is paved with good intentions because good intentions have never changed anything. Something much more profound is needed: to *act together* for the right reason, not just to think the right thoughts.

There is a tragic war to stop, not because we aren't patriotic but because we are more than patriotic—we are compassionate. There is a cancerous greed on the corporate body of the land that is so corrupt that it threatens free enterprise itself, and we prefer to save it rather than let it self-destruct. There is a set of values at work in the halls of power today that is so self-serving and so antithetical to the core values of this great country that we can no longer be silent.

The time has come for people of good conscience everywhere to act on their feelings of frustration and betrayal about the direction of this country. We do not have to agree on every issue, and we certainly should not adopt the tactics of those who have seized power. But we must resist them in ways that actually compromise that power—*take it back* and begin to disassemble the assumptions and the resources that make it possible. Because there were no weapons of mass destruction and no imminent threat, we must now become an imminent threat to the future of the Christian Right and its political machine. We can do this by *constant, unrelenting, proactive* engagement with a world whose future we have forfeited to others. We must question everything again—assumptions, methods, and the underlying premises that we are made happy by consuming and that the way to be respected is to be feared.

The next generation must confront the inevitable lessons of history. There would have been no end to slavery without a civil war, no successful civil rights movement without a "Bloody Sunday" on the Edmund Pettus Bridge between Selma and Montgomery. The battle for inclusion must now be waged courageously and faithfully, whether inside the church or outside it. Little hope exists for saving the environment until indignant people realize that we all live downstream and start marching upstream en masse. The prophet Micah gave us our marching orders long ago when he asked, "What does the Lord require of [us] but to do justice, love kindness, and walk humbly with our God?" (6–8).

Faith is not about believing certain things but about doing what needs to be done to build the Kingdom on earth. *Faith* is a noun to the grammarian, but in its deepest, truest form, it is a *verb* to the disciple—and an action verb at that. Doing justice cannot be separated from hating injustice; loving kindness cannot be separated from despising cruelty; and walking humbly with God still requires us to stand up and walk!

Remember, to be indignant is not to lose one's dignity. What we need, now more than ever, are communities of dignified indignance. We need to consciously seek out and work to develop networks of like-minded citizens who will join us in the struggle for peace and justice. Where these communities exist, we should join them. Where they do not exist, we should create them. This means, first of all, that we will have to get over our aversion to the idea of community itself. The oldest maxim for taking and holding power is "divide and conquer," and the Right has perfected it in our time. If America remains a collection of individuals striving against other individuals, our voice will never be heard. To resist, we must also unite.

Communities require sacrifice. They don't form themselves without human effort, a shared vision, organizational structure, and the experience that almost every busy person wants to avoid these days: another meeting. Forming such communities and then supporting them is not unlike the hard work that other covenants require: marriage, family, good neighborhood, good schools.

But this much is certain. Collective resistance is an essential component of social change. People need to know that other people feel as they do and are willing to make the effort to do something about it. We need to get together and encourage one another, because the leading cause of resignation is burnout, and this is often the result of feeling isolated. The Right is happy to have a nation of competitors, whether for profits or for social change. They fear communities of resistance for exactly the same reason they fear unions: collective power.

We can no longer afford to live apart from one another. We can no longer consider society to be a collection of millions of individual "self-help" projects striving for the good life without mutual sacrifice and a shared vision. Communities of dignified indignance do not have to be religious, and they do not have to be large or well financed. But they must be *organized* and clear in their goals. They can meet in schools, in libraries, in restaurants, or in homes, but they must meet—and meet regularly.

As for dignified indignance, it is not an oxymoron. It is the most powerful force in the universe. It drove the British from India and defeated the forces of hatred in the civil rights movement. It has accompanied countless saints to jail and comforted countless martyrs who faced death rather than abandon their conscience. Nonviolent social change will do no harm where harm can be avoided and is committed to fearless resistance after the example of Jesus and Gandhi.

Pacifists and nonpacifists can engage in such resistance. It is not just a call to public demonstrations or voluntary arrest but also to private transformation that becomes an example to the next generation. Parents need to teach peace and live peace in front of their children. Teachers and other role models need to teach tolerance and nonviolence. But that's not all. When we live in critical times, we must also learn *how* to resist. This can be done in many ways, as long as we are committed to the cause, as long as we encourage one another, and as long as we first consider exactly what it is we are up against.

One of the most important and most overlooked dimensions of resistance is the idea of noncooperation. Our elected officials draw their power from the consent of the people. Retailers and advertisers are given permission to define human happiness so long as we sanction their work by buying their products. Preachers are empowered to peddle bad theology, divide the House of God, and preach hatred so long as parishioners are so uninformed about their own Gospel that they do not know when to get up and walk out of the sanctuary. Presidents can violate every principle of leadership and unleash death and destruction through stupidity and arrogance only so long as we permit it by failing to be informed, to think critically, and to vote. One thing is certain: when the idealists among us drop out or tune out, those in power gain even more power. The result is that we get exactly the kind of government we deserve.

What we need now is a plan of action, a simple guide to constructive, nonviolent resistance. Instead of worn-out labels and endless political diatribes, we need a new, diverse coalition of Americans who will agree to become practitioners of nonviolent social change in at least five critical areas: (1) the antiwar movement, (2) the movement to reconstruct a hapless Democratic Party, (3) the Green movement to protect the environment, (4) the "use less stuff" consumer movement, and (5) the Sermon on the Mount movement, lest Jesus remain captive and muzzled.

Make Levees, Not War

MAKE LEVEES, NOT WAR is more than just a clever slogan spotted at an antiwar rally in Washington, D.C. It is a reminder that choices matter and that our national priorities are not just skewed but have deadly consequences. Money spent for the war takes money away from important local projects like building stronger levees in New Orleans. A government's first responsibility is to protect its own citizens, not to engage in wars of choice without a clear mission or to defend us against imaginary threats.

Whether or not it is ever moral to fight a war is the subject of endless debate, and the church has struggled to justify wars of last resort as "just wars."[2] But the war in Iraq was chosen and violates many of the tenets of just-war theory. The first criterion, for example, is *just cause:* force may be used only to correct a grave public evil, such as a massive violation of the basic rights of whole populations. In the case of Iraq, atrocities had been committed by Saddam Hussein against portions of the population, but mass genocide was not under way.

Another criterion of a just war is *right intention:* force may be used only in a truly just cause and solely for that purpose; correcting a suffered wrong is considered a right intention, while material gain is not. In the case of Iraq, no American had been killed in Iraq prior to the war, and it is widely believed that controlling the flow of oil from the region was a major factor in the decision to invade.

Yet another key element of just-war theory is *proportionality:* the overall destruction expected from the use of force must be outweighed by the good to be achieved. In the case of Iraq, the massive destruction of an already war-ravaged country has been outweighed by almost no good results whatsoever. Iraqis have voted in U.S.-run elections, but the forced nature of those elections and the continued violence among ethnic and religious factions in the country have caused even more violence and brought the country to the brink of civil war.

One of the most important components of just-war theory, however, is *last resort:* force may be used only after all peaceful and viable alternatives have been seriously tried and exhausted. Though Saddam often frustrated them, peaceful inspections were ongoing, and one of the enduring media myths of this war is that the inspectors were "kicked out" of Iraq. In fact, Bush called them home in order to mount his invasion. Iraq had violated numerous UN sanctions, but it possessed no weapons capable of threatening anyone in the region and thus was not an imminent threat to anyone. Iraq had not invaded another country, nor was it threatening to do so. Absent the justification that all peaceful efforts had failed, the invasion of Iraq was clearly a violation of international law rather than a war of last resort.

In conducting a just war, one of the most important considerations is that "acts of war should be directed toward those who inflicted the wrong and not toward civilians caught in circumstances they did not create." The more disproportional the number of collateral civilian deaths, the more suspect is the claim that the one who initiated the war is conducting the war justly. Under no circumstances, according to just-war theory, should prisoners of war be tortured.

Now the deadly quagmire that so many feared is a grim reality. The war has no noble purpose that can justify the sacrifice of our soldiers. We are laying waste to civilian populations and turning Iraq into a training ground for anti-Western terrorists. The latest reason given for the war, that we are establishing democracy in Iraq, would require a first in human history, for no democracy has ever been established by an ongoing military occupation beset by a fierce insurgency. "It is dangerous hubris to believe we can build other nations."[3]

The only problem is that once you have sacrificed the lives of so many Americans, what do you tell the parents of dead soldiers that their loved ones died for? Insisting that we must not "cut and run," the administration is exhibiting the same macho intransigence that got us into the war and prevents it from admitting its tragic mistake and bringing the troops home. But this is the same deadly error we made in Vietnam, and we are watching it play out all over again. The premise of that war was also a deception, as former Secretary of Defense Robert MacNamara has now admitted, and yet the slaughter went on for another decade. Every politician in those days who ran on the promise to "end the war and bring the troops home" was called "soft on communism" or accused of "dishonoring the sacrifice of our heroes." The strategy of divide and conquer kept them out of office and tragically extended the futile deaths of tens of thousands of members of my own generation. The question then, as it is now, was not when we bring the troops home but how many of them will make it home alive or in one piece.

This is what Cindy Sheehan understood when she camped out for a month along the road to the president's Texas ranch in the summer of 2005 and refused to leave until he would agree to meet with her. Her son Casey was killed in Sadr City in April 2004, at the age of twenty-four. Like all those who have died in Iraq, the nation refers to him as a "fallen hero" and urges us on lest we fail all those like him who have made the ultimate sacrifice. Therefore, in a vicious cycle of deadly redundancy, an honorable death in a dishonorable war becomes the rationale for more death in a war that is still dishonorable.

The mother of a dead soldier deserves to be heard, and her cry was the disturbing intrusion of a painful truth upon a carefully choreographed lie. She decided that the emperor was naked, and the myth could only deprive more mothers of their sons. Camped outside the ranch of a president who takes his vacations very seriously and whose own daughters are not and will never be in harm's way, she became the symbol of the parallel universes in which we live. She wanted to ask the president a simple question: "For what noble purpose did my son die?" For this she was vilified by the Right for changing her mind about the war and making an embarrassing public spectacle on which the media could feast. She is not an antiwar protester, railed Rush Limbaugh on his radio program, but an "anti-American protester."

So it has come to this, as it always does. Those who try to stop war are portrayed as unpatriotic, weak, and dismissive of the ultimate sacrifice that has already been made. But this is a lie as deep and deadly as the lies that led us into the war. Cindy Sheehan was not a publicity hound. She's a mother who lost her child. She decided that the truly patriotic thing to do was to try to hasten the end of the war in any way she could so that other mothers would not have to welcome their sons or daughters home in flag-draped coffins.

It's up to all of us to stop it now. We can do this by bringing constant, punitive pressure on every elected official who supports the war. When the march comes to your hometown, put on your walking shoes and go. When the chance to write a letter comes, write it. Then write another one and another one. You may get a form letter back, but politicians do notice mail when it reaches a certain volume. There are numerous Web sites like http://www.house.gov and http://www

.senate.gov where you can find the names, phone numbers, fax numbers, and mailing addresses for your elected representatives. Go to http://www.stopwar.org to get links to numerous antiwar Web sites and practical suggestions for things you can do to protest the war.

When you hear a discussion about the war, at work, in the marketplace, among your friends, do not shrink from challenging rationales that are not backed up by the facts. Many conservatives now have deep misgivings about the war, as do many thoughtful evangelicals. Give them a chance to oppose the war in their own way and to challenge the notion that we are all "constituents in a box." The coalitions we form now must be broad and deep, and we will have to agree to disagree about some things in order to accomplish what we all can agree on. This war must end.

Even if you are not a member of a church or active in some community of faith, take the time to educate yourself on just-war theory so that you can challenge religious rationales for the war. Sometimes the painful truth comes from the outside, calling to the church through an open window. Asking, "Who would Jesus bomb?" is not a childish question, just a very difficult one to answer.

The military is running out of recruits, and the Reserve and National Guard forces now make up about 40 percent of the troops in Iraq—often forced to remain beyond their tour of duty in a kind of backdoor draft. Most military experts now believe that there will soon be insufficient troops to accomplish the missions in Afghanistan and Iraq without an increase in the size of the armed forces. That can only be accomplished by reinstating the draft, which seems politically untenable, or by drawing other nations into the war on our side. During the Vietnam era, some asked the question, "What if they gave a war and no one came?" Perhaps we are close to finding out.

That is, unless the military continues to expand its presence in K–12 schools, where it is now allowed more freedom to propagandize students with promises of money for college and military service as a kind of travel adventure to exotic ports of call. The recruiting techniques are now so sophisticated and, at their core, so dishonest that no antiwar movement can ignore the importance of "counterrecruitment activism"[4] in our schools. Parents need to insist that their schools are not just drug-free zones but also military-free zones. High school graduates and their parents can explore military options by going to a recruiting station. The recruiting station should not be brought to the school.

Military recruiters use powerful messages of glamour and glory to persuade impressionable young people that they should enlist. We must do a better job of offering alternatives to enlistment, such as job-training programs and college scholarships. By doing so, we can materially interfere with the ability of the government to sustain its unjust occupation of Iraq and discourage our leaders from considering other preemptive wars. We should petition to have the so-called Solomon Amendments overturned, which threaten college campuses with the loss of federal funds if they ban recruiters and ROTC representatives. A similar law forbids schools from restricting recruiter access to students and student lists. During Vietnam, every eighteen-year-old male had to register with the draft board. Now every high school senior's name is made available to military recruiters.

The key to success in stopping this war is to collectively withdraw our consent. We must stop consenting to improper military recruitment. We must stop consenting to the budget cuts caused by military expenditures. We must apply economic pressure on corporations that profit from war by boycotting the civilian products they make. We must stop consenting to an "us against them" mentality by refusing to let nationalism and jingoism go unchallenged or "my country right or wrong" definitions of patriotism go unanswered.

In ways big and small, we must "make trouble" for the warmaking machinery of the country we love. Nonviolent resistance requires sacrifice and suffering, and we seem to have lost our capacity to give up anything for the greater good. When enough people demonstrate that they are willing to resist at the risk of their own liberty, treasure, and reputation, the world will take notice. Until we do more than simply gather in large numbers with other like-minded folk, the Bush administration will consider us just one more "focus group." It will even remind everyone that this is the "freedom of expression that our brave men and women are fighting for."

We can't just shout, "No blood for oil!" We have to *use* less oil. We can't just say, "Bring the troops home!" We have to cut off the supply of young people who are persuaded to go in the first place. We can't just throw verbal poison darts at those who believe they are fighting terrorism the only way they believe it can be fought. We have to articulate another way of fighting it.

When Martin Luther King Jr. called on all Americans to conduct the struggle for peace and justice "on the high plane of dignity and discipline," he did not mean to suggest that we would not suffer or sacrifice. He said we must do both with our heads held high and without violence, "meeting physical force with soul force."[5] From the pulpit of New York's Riverside Church in 1967, in a speech called "Beyond Vietnam," King called on all Americans to create a world where people are more important than profit motives and property rights, to "rapidly begin the shift from a thing-oriented society to a person-oriented society."[6] If we fail to do this, King said, we will never stop marching because there will never be justice.

Will the Real Democrats Please Stand Up?

I am old enough to remember when Democrats were Democrats. They stood solidly behind working people and protected the weak from the ravages of the strong. They knew that unions were a necessary evil to protect the middle class and that the marketplace does not solve all the problems of life. They believed in the minimum wage, a safe shop, clean water, independent churches, and a strong defense. They remembered the Great Depression and were vigilant about the dangers of too much wealth and too much power falling into too few hands. They distrusted big business, fought for the American farmer, and prayed to Jesus privately. They believed in hard work, family values, and defending America against "all enemies, foreign or domestic." They were blue-collar, mainstream, and deeply religious.

Not so long ago, these Democrats owned the Deep South, and politicians could count on southern Democrats the way the Republican can now count on—well, southern Democrats! What happened, of course, was the civil rights movement and the disaffection of the southern white male. Nixon was the first to employ the so-called southern strategy, which used race as a wedge issue, to win over anxious white working stiffs. It was so successful that today's Republican Party is still doing it, only now the issues are homosexuality, the moral depravity of the elites, un-Christian art, improper flag displays, and creeping liberalism. The Great Backlash, which political satirist Thomas Frank describes in his insightful book *What's the Matter with Kansas?* has truly turned the world upside down.[7]

Now, in order to save the country from a host of imaginary evils, the poorest Americans vote against their own economic self-interest and seem more fervently committed to the Republican agenda than society's winners are. How did this happen? The backlash is the cleverest bait-and-switch scheme to come along since the Trojan Horse. While systematically downplaying economic issues and focusing on "values," the preachers and pundits of the Right work average people into an apocalyptic fury. Once the votes are secured, Republican politicians go to work on the real agenda: low wages, lax business and environmental regulations, and cutting taxes on the wealthy. Frank put it perfectly: "The leaders of the backlash may talk Christ, but they walk corporate. Values may 'matter most' to voters, but they always take a backseat to the needs of money once the elections are won."[8]

Oddly enough, both the great political parties in America need to return to their roots. The Democrats, now more than ever, need to stand with workers and protect them from a return to the economic conditions of the nineteenth century. Republicans need to recover their Grand Old Party identity and stop pretending that they are God's Own Party. The revival tactics of fundamentalist preachers may seem irresistible to politicians, frightening people into selling their souls to a savior in the culture wars, but the traditional principles of conservatism are all being betrayed by this unholy alliance with the Christian Right. Instead of limited government and fiscal responsibility, we now have a federal government that is out of control and free to intrude into the most personal, private areas of life.

The deadly mistake of my beleaguered Democrats is that they tried to ride the Republican horse with a softer saddle. Democrats pretending to be "Republican Lite" have only solidified the power of the extreme Right by abdicating their position as a true opposition party. As middle-class Americans have watched their incomes stagnate, even working two or three jobs, and seen small towns dry up and blow away as manufacturing jobs were "outsourced" in the name of free trade, Democrats have answered with a deafening whimper. Their message often sounds like a dull lecture, a bloodless resolution written by a policy wonk using long compound-complex sentences and words like *enabled* and *empowered*. Meanwhile, the Republicans are leading an altar call with God, guns, and guts.

If the Democrats want to reinvent themselves, if they want to *resist* the choreographed media sideshow that modern politics has become, they must begin with an old idea: government "of the people, by the people, and for the people—so help us *God*." That's right, as difficult as it is for modern Democrats to talk about faith, the truth is that their own party's history of fighting for those who are left out and protecting those who are powerless is in fact one long, tortured, inspired act of *faith*.

Democrats don't all have to be Christians, of course, but the Christians who are Democrats had better learn to explain why Jesus still matters and why any attempt to use his name to divide and conquer is a sin. Instead of leaving religious rhetoric to nonpractitioners, the new Democrats will have to be the old Democrats, immortalized by the spirit of Jim Casey, the former preacher turned Universalist in John Steinbeck's *Grapes of Wrath*. He saw through all the phoniness of organized religion in a way that makes this Okie proud and decided that God was bigger than anyone realized and that "holiness" was about the way everything is connected to everything else—not about how we pray but about how we care for one another.

When the Joad family asks him to pray at breakfast, he explains that his old beliefs about God are dead. "Maybe there ain't no sin and there ain't no virtue, they's just what people does. Some things folks do is nice and some ain't so nice, and that's all any man's got a right to say."[9]

Would that such humility were the mark of religion in our time. Instead, the one "religious" figure in Steinbeck's novel bears a striking resemblance to what passes for religion in our time. She is Mrs. Sandy, a fanatic who condemns everyone in the government camp as a sinner. She condemns dancing, music, and theater as the vilest of sins and warns that God's retribution will be harsh. Sound familiar?

The call to resistance in our time is not a call to abandon either faith or politics but rather one to remember on whose behalf the faithful have always labored. Prayer breakfasts are not enough, nor are megachurches that offer Christian aerobics and Happy Meals for Jesus. Just as prayer was not enough to ease the burden of the Okie migrants, neither is the phony rhetoric of "compassionate conservatism" enough to lift millions out of poverty. Casey decides that the most religious thing he can do is form a union, because "without us, God will not; without God, we cannot." They need leadership to solve their problems, not more advice about how "God helps those who help themselves." In the end, Casey is murdered for standing with the poor. If that makes him a Christ figure, so be it. Perhaps, indeed, we all need to revisit exactly what a Christ figure would look like if we met one. Christ figures do not live for the rich. They die for the poor.

In the meantime, it will be up to all of us to resist organized religion when it becomes manipulative and oppressive. The perversion of faith as a instrument of power is the perversion of religion itself. Democrats will have to recover not only their own soul but also their ability to talk about the soul of faith itself, which is about loving one's neighbor as oneself, not about condemning the neighbor while trying to serve both God and mammon.

The Democrats will have to say, plainly and with passion, that we are *for* universal heath care, and Jesus would be too. That we are *for* a living wage, and Jesus would be too. That we invented "family values" by giving the country a forty-hour workweek, laws against child labor, and Social Security—so that everyone's family, and not just ours, could live in dignity. When the Right calls us "liberals," we should smile and say thank you. As retired Lutheran pastor Daniel Bruch put it, "I don't know if Jesus was the first liberal, but he was an important one."[10]

We are the party that believes the government should not restrict personal freedom but increase it, not spend our children's money but save it, turn our backs not on the poor but on the rampant individualism that is undermining the American dream. We are the party that believes in plurality, tolerance, and the separation of church and state. We love Jesus the Jew, but also all Jews, Muslims, Hindus, Sikhs, Buddhists, and those wonderful pagans. Is this a recipe for disaster? No, it's our only hope of survival.

Thomas Frank put it this way: "American conservatism depends for its continued dominance and even for its very existence on people never making certain mental connections about the world, connections that until recently were treated as obvious or self-evident everywhere on the planet."[11] In other words, the disconnect between religious rhetoric and public policy depends on *mindlessness*. If we are going to take back this country and the church, we will have to swear off something much more frightening than being soft on sin. We will have to agree that there is absolutely nothing endearing about ignorance—only something deadly.

Red, White, and Green

As prodemocracy movements have spread around the world, people who are resisting various forms of totalitarianism have adopted various colors to mark their cause. In the former Yugoslavia, the "power of the people" movement was Orange Power. Throughout the Cold War, Americans said, "Better dead than Red." When we wear black armbands, we make one statement; when we wear rainbow flags, we make another. Ribbons of various colors are omnipresent in America and signify favored causes: curing breast cancer, supporting the troops, ending child abuse. As a nation, we love to color-code our "identity politics." But there is one color that now means more to the survival of the human race than any other: green.

I'm not talking about the Green Party or what Rush Limbaugh loves to call "tree huggers" but rather about a larger, more diverse movement that understands the urgency of living differently on the planet, lest we destroy it. This is a movement that must transcend politics but unfortunately does not. The Christian Right is not leading us toward a sustainable environmental policy, and the political Right it has energized has nothing but disdain for environmentalists who stand in the way of profits by putting limits on human activity. The Right's excuse is God's call in Scripture to "be fruitful and multiply, and fill the earth and subdue it" (Genesis 1:28).

But those words were written when human survival was at stake, and the earth did not groan under the weight of more than six billion inhabitants. We have subdued it, already—almost to death! Now it would seem that the earth itself is fighting back. Few events have so dramatically demonstrated the effects of global warming as the massive hurricanes that hit the Gulf Coast in 2005. Hurricanes get their energy from warm ocean waters, and the gulf water has never been warmer. Scientific journals report that the proportion of hurricanes that reach category 4 or 5 has almost doubled since the 1970s.[12] After the president pulled us out of the Kyoto accord to protect American companies, we learned that the expense of reducing global warming is actually far less that the cost of weather-related losses that are now predicted. One study indicated that global warming could be cut by one-third for a cost equal to one-tenth of 1 percent of worldwide gross domestic product.[13] Local and state governments are starting to act on their own, and citizens can join them. One of the defining acts of conscience is to sacrifice something for a day you will never see and to plant seeds that you will never harvest. When it comes to "being green," resistance can take many forms.

To begin with, we must stop thinking that concern for the environment is a partisan issue or that companies can't do business, make profits, and also protect the earth. When politicians don't make concrete environmental policy promises, don't vote for them. If they make environmental promises they don't keep, don't reelect them. At all levels of government, hold public officials accountable for environmental quality, commitment to renewable energy, and support for sustainable farming. When corporate farming entities come to your community—giant hog farms or warehouse poultry operations, for example—reject them on environmental grounds. In Oklahoma and Arkansas, corporate farms have been environmental disasters. Family farmers are better stewards of the land.

Teach your children to regard the land as a living thing, an ecosystem of which we are a part, not a commodity that belongs to us. For the same reason that you should never park your car in a handicapped space without a permit, neither should you dump your engine oil in an empty lot or put paint thinner or other banned materials in your curbside trash. Environmental ethics begin at home.

Some important environmental efforts can be collective as well as individual. Supporting local farmer's markets and organically grown food is a simple way to reduce the distance that food must travel. Community-supported agriculture is an increasingly popular way to purchase groceries through co-ops. The idea is to support local growers and connect consumers again to food grown in their own area that is minimally packaged and sold in bulk. It's all about "sustainabilty."

Think of everything in the world as part of a system that has an effect on every other thing in every other part of the system. Recycle everything you can, and don't buy electrical appliances to do things you can easily do by hand (like opening cans). Use cold water to wash with whenever possible, and reuse the bags you buy, avoiding plastic. Use food containers for storage instead of plastic wrap or aluminum foil. Save wire coat hangers and return them to the cleaners. Take out everything you haven't worn in your closet for one year and give it to charity. Don't leave water running, even when you brush your teeth. Turn the heat down and wear a sweater, and do what you tell your kids to do—turn out the lights when you leave a room. Conserve water by flushing less often, and turn off your water heater when you go on vacation. Recycle your Christmas tree.

You can practice environmental stewardship in your own yard by avoiding the "perfect lawn syndrome" and opting for low-maintenance plantings. You can start your own compost pile, feed the birds, pull weeds instead of using herbicides, and avoid lawn services that spray chemicals all over your neighborhood. Whenever possible, use organic fertilizer.

Buy smaller, more fuel-efficient cars, keep them tuned, and use public transportation or carpool whenever possible. Walking or riding a bike is still one of the purest forms of recreation and facilitates both meditation and weight loss. Take your engine oil to a recycling center, and never litter the roads and highways. It is always astonishing to me that people in cars covered in Christian bumper stickers will empty their ashtrays onto the street at a stoplight and then just drive away.

At work, you can recycle office and computer paper and reuse paper whenever possible. One the simplest things you can do is make copies on both sides of the paper and reuse envelopes and file folders. Banish Styrofoam cups; have each person bring a coffee mug that can be washed and reused. When you are shopping, try to avoid "disposable" products because they really aren't disposable, and buy paper products instead of plastic. Buy energy-efficient appliances, and support local food producers, especially those who grow organically. Buy fewer meat and animal products and more fruits and vegetables.

The way we treat the earth speaks volumes about our true regard for our neighbors and for our understanding of what is holy and transcendent. The fact that the most ardently "Christian" administration ever has also compiled the worst environmental record is not an accident. Bad theology makes for bad policy.

Some scholars believe that because Christianity is the most anthropocentric religion in the world, we often think of ourselves as both privileged and "just passing through." The monotheism that replaced the gods, spirits, and demons of the pagan world also removed the idea of sacredness from the natural world and posited a God who was supernatural, removed from nature, and separate from the world. In a sense, by understanding the cosmos as a layered "three-story universe," we have unwittingly secularized the world by stripping it of its intrinsic holiness.

What's more, a closed religious system like fundamentalist Christianity does not admit to the idea that we should learn from other cultures and belief systems—rather, they should conform to ours. Americans have always considered themselves to be the apple of God's eye, and our conquest of native peoples was the fulfillment of "manifest destiny." Ronald Reagan, who said in 1981 that "trees cause more pollution than automobiles do," went so far as to say that God had placed this land "between the two great oceans to be found by special people from every corner of the world who had that extra love of freedom that prompted them to leave their homeland and come to this land to make it a brilliant light beam of freedom to the world."[14]

This lack of humility, this notion that God favors us and justifies whatever we are up to, has caused us to exploit the natural world rather than live in harmony with it. We are not distinct from the luminous web of life but part of its interlocking strands. Human beings did not come down from the sky but up from the sea, and our DNA is a composite of all life forms, not some new and superior manifestation. Our way of living on the earth and our way of relating to all living things are therefore tests of our true faith.

The wise preacher in Ecclesiastes reminds his readers that "the fate of the sons of men and the fate of beasts is the same. . . . They all have the same breath, and man has no advantage over the beasts" (3:19). If this is true, we have many changes to make and not much time to make them. If the world is going to survive and keep all its colors, the rest of us are going to have to be green.

Use Less Stuff

After all is said and done, after every argument is made, after ever strident voice has fallen silent, these three little words may be the last, best hope we have. Here is a message that can't be misunderstood. It calls us to a simpler, saner life in a world that has gone mad in pursuit of material possessions. It cuts through the noisy racket of politics, the stained-glass voice of preachers, and the slick artistry of the ad man. It suggests something so simple yet so radical that it sounds almost un-American. It may be the most effective form of resistance there is. Call it "downward mobility."

We are a nation of consumers, "born to shop," caught in an endless spiral of buying and then throwing away what the culture tells us we just "have to have." The message is constant, the tactics are ingenious, the appeal is quasi-religious: *we are what we own.*

But most of what we own is useless, a mountain of plastic so flimsy and transient that it moves from the package to the landfill in the blink of an eye. If it's true, as theologian Paul Tillich once said, that whatever is of "ultimate concern" to us is what we worship,[15] then in America we worship stuff.

Witness the almost depressing spectacle on the day after Thanksgiving when people line up by the hundreds outside the "big box" stores waiting for the doors to open in the predawn darkness so that they can rush in and begin shopping. They are driven by such a frenzy that they often knock one another down, and someone always gets hurt. What drives them to such a frenzy? Stuff.

The stuff that will go into our homes and then, when there is not enough room for all of it, get crammed into the garage. Finally, when the garage is full, we will rent a storage unit or two. Then we will go to estate sales, garage sales, and special year-end clearance sales to buy more stuff. And all of it, absolutely all of it, will eventually be garbage. Every single artifact that we covet, every stick of furniture, every electronic gadget, every big-screen TV is headed for the dump.

There are things we need, of course, and things we desire, but our ability to know the difference between them (which is the wisdom of Buddhism) seems conspicuously absent. My generation, the "money can't buy me love" crowd, has become the most materialistic generation of all time. Our idolatry of stuff borders on the fanatical. Our houses have become huge. Our cars are like suburban tanks. Our closets are bigger than our parents' bedrooms. Our bathrooms are Roman spas. We love our stuff. But our stuff does not love us back.

In fact, our stuff is killing us. It is being used to fill the spaces that are intended for what is holy. Henri Nouwen once said that the spiritual life is about "holding open empty space" so that there is a vacancy for the spirit.[16] But we stuff ourselves so full of our stuff that there is no vacancy, just a perpetual hunger. Late at night, when we can't sleep, we turn on the television, and there are plenty of preachers. So we listen, hoping for a word of grace, a word of honesty, a word from God. And what do we see, what do we hear? Beautifully adorned people, coiffed and confident, sitting in gilded studios talking about a God who is a cross between a personal trainer and an investment counselor. The message from the preacher is indistinguishable from the advertisements that surround it: *whatever you want, God wants you to have it.*

As America has grown more conservative and reassured itself that we are in the midst of a great revival, the line between church and state has been blurred, but also the line between church and commerce. Millionaires and billionaires run the country now, and they all say they love Jesus. But nobody can really tell the difference anymore between a disciple and a customer. It used to be that you could spot followers of Jesus because they traveled light and taught nonviolence. They embraced radical hospitality and welcomed strangers. They lived the itinerant life, believing that bread and love could sustain them. They got along with less. We always want more.

If we are going to join, or create, communities of dignified indignance, the first thing we are going to have to do is fall out of love with our stuff. We can resist by living more simply, by withdrawing the consent of our dollars, by consuming with the knowledge that the future is something we have borrowed from our children.

Big cars and the war in Iraq really do have something in common. Mansions and the shedding of blood in the desert sand really are connected in the deadly mutuality of excess. The "lifestyles of the rich and famous" are made possible by the sacrifice of the poor and the unknown. Perhaps instead of saying that our stuff is killing us, we should first admit that other people are literally dying for it.

Greed steals bread in a world where there are only so many loaves. We can no longer afford to be oblivious.

One of the most powerful ways that a person can resist the madness of our time is to recognize that living simply makes a powerful statement in a world that worships material possessions. Taking only what you need, sharing more of what you have, and shunning all that is just for show will not just lighten the load. It will illuminate your soul. Stuff makes heavy demands on us—and piles up between us and the things that really matter.

In an age of prosperity theology, born-again billionaires, and disdain for the quaint concept of conservation, using less stuff is one way to distinguish yourself from the dominant culture. When you make do with less, the world will notice, and people will ask you why you don't want more. Tell them you are *content*, which is one of the manifestations of peace. It is a constant striving for more that characterizes people who are not living comfortably within their own skin or connected to anything more important than the stock market. Simple living is radical living.

Of all the presidents in living memory, most people would agree that Jimmy Carter is the most admired for his humble but transforming faith. He has taught Sunday school all his life and still does. He talks openly of his faith, but he also believes passionately in the separation of church and state. He was a committed evangelical but not a fundamentalist. The difference between the lifestyles and priorities of Jimmy Carter and George W. Bush could not be more dramatic. Carter talked openly about conservation during the 1974 oil embargo and turned down the thermostats in the White House and wore sweaters, for which he was mercilessly parodied. He rejected the imperial presidency and then spent his postpresidential years among some of the poorest people on the planet. He was active in the founding of Habitat for Humanity and has been an unrepentant crusader for human rights.

Although Jimmy Carter was the first American president to speak openly about being "born again," which was quite a novelty in 1976, he never wore his religion on his sleeve, nor did he use the language of faith to vilify or demonize the "evildoers" in the world. Jimmy Carter considered faith to be a deeply private but transforming force in life, even as he respected the beliefs of others. In a memorable interview with *Playboy* magazine, Carter confessed to having "lusted in his heart" on occasion when he looked at a beautiful woman. The Right lambasted him for speech "unbecoming of a president." His crime: telling the truth. In the church, we used to call that *confession*.

With the imperial presidency has come an imperial Christianity. Perhaps we should all take a class from the Quakers again, whose emphasis on simplicity, or what they called *plainness*, would make it possible for us all to use less stuff. Early Friends believed that fanciness in dress, speech, and material possessions detracted from the spiritual life. They limited their possessions to what they needed to live, rather than accumulating luxuries. It was not just the *nature* of one's possessions that was a problem but rather the *attitude* toward these material goods. Simplicity of dress, of speech, and of daily living was what set them apart from others.

There is just something positively ludicrous about fantastically wealthy men and women giving "all the glory" to a penniless rabbi from Nazareth—and it's time we all said so. If religion makes us more selfish or just baptizes the selfishness that is natural to the human condition, we would be better off without it. But if it drives us back on ourselves and back to Walden Pond, then it would be a miracle in this new Gilded Age.

The man who deliberately journeyed into simplicity and then wrote it about most eloquently was Henry David Thoreau. "I went to the woods," he said, "because I wished to live deliberately, to front only the essential facts of life, and see if I could not learn what it had to teach, and not, when I came to die, discover that I had not lived."[17]

It was Thoreau who advised us to march to a different drummer and to "beware of all enterprises that require new clothes." He confessed once that "an early morning walk is a blessing for the whole day" and that he had "never found a companion that was so companionable as solitude." Yet it was not a withdrawal from the world, in the end, that Thoreau is advising but a withdrawal from vanity for the sake of sanity. "Our life is frittered away by detail . . . ," he wrote. "Simplify, simplify."[18]

He knew that those who are not comfortable "alone with themselves" and their "pretty toys" can be the most lonely and dangerous people on earth. In a chilling prophecy of the ecological disaster that was to come he wrote, "If a man walks in the woods for love of them half of each day, he is in danger of being regarded as a loafer. But if he spends his days as a speculator, shearing off those woods and making the earth bald before her time, he is deemed an industrious and enterprising citizen. . . . To have done anything just for money is to have been truly idle."[19]

Let us not forget that it was Thoreau who taught us about the true meaning of civil disobedience, and his lessons were an inspiration to Gandhi. It was Thoreau who made this seminal statement: "If the machine of government is of such a nature that it requires you to be the agent of injustice to another, then, I say, break the law." When he refused to pay a tax to, or recognize the authority of, the state, "which buys and sells men, women, and children, like cattle, at the door of its senate-house," he was arrested and thrown in jail. When his friend Ralph Waldo Emerson came to visit him, Emerson reportedly asked, "Henry, what are you doing in there?" to which Thoreau responded with dignified indignance, "Waldo, the question is what are you doing out there?"[20]

We Want Jesus Back

One of the most amazing things about the response to my antiwar speech is that so many of the most heartfelt letters of gratitude came from non-Christians. In language that was almost apologetic, people from every conceivable theological and philosophical point of view wrote to say that they wanted to join the struggle, but first they had to say up front that they could not do so as part of organized religion. They know that I am a minister, but they also wanted to know if nonbelievers could do something to help. It felt to me like a vast congregation in exile, a Diaspora of social justice types who have given up on organized religion (and not without good reason) but refuse to give up on justice.

They were either not Christians (but part of Abraham's original family, the Jews, or his extended family, the Muslims) or atheists, agnostics, pagans, Unitarians, lapsed Catholics, lapsed Pentecostals, witches, Druids, even former members of the Weather Underground. They were physicians who heal but don't go to church, teachers who teach but can't stand mindless preachers, and a host of strangers, "others" from every nation under heaven: "Parthians, Medes, Elamites, and residents of Mesopotamia, Judea and Cappadocia, Pontus and Asia, Phrygia and Pamphylia, Egypt and the part of Libya belonging to Cyrene, and visitors from Rome, both Jews and proselytes . . ." (Acts 2:9–10). And let's not forget the Cretans—the ones your mother warned you about.

What was amazing to me about all the letters I received wasn't that they were mad as hell at the Bush administration. Nor was I surprised by the depth of their despair over the war, the deficit, or the audacity of the claim by the Christian Right to have cornered the market on "morality." The amazing thing to me about this diverse group of people, churched and unchurched alike, was how much they *miss Jesus!* How much they want him back. How *incensed* they are, even if they are not believers, that the Jesus of history, the Prince of Peace, the Teacher of the alternative wisdom of the Sermon on the Mount, has been hijacked by people who talk about him all the time but seem totally devoid of his influence. What else are we to make of Jerry Falwell's boast that "God is pro-war"?[21]

It's as if the people who are supposed to know him don't know him anymore and the people who shouldn't care still do. Perhaps now, as in the first century, we have come to another moment when the keepers of our religious traditions are no longer seen as worthy of that responsibility. They know the name of Jesus, but they don't recognize his face. They enjoy appealing to him for everything under the sun, but if they met him on a lonely road, he would startle them.

If they engaged him in conversation unaware, like the disciples who met a stranger on the road to Emmaus, they might not even invite him to stay.

But now I understand better what all these people are saying to me, even if their voices are coming from outside the walls. Many of them do not believe that they abandoned the church but rather that the church abandoned them. They go through each day with both a primal memory (that we are from God and to God) and a deep and festering wound from organized religion that will not heal. Long ago, they stopped believing in things they know are not true, but they cannot dislodge images from the gallery of their hearts—like the gentle shepherd, carrying one lost sheep over his shoulder. Long after we have quit caring about Trinitarian debates, a white dove remains in our memory, descending from heaven above a young, bearded man standing waist deep in the muddy waters of the Jordan.

In the old wedding ceremonies, there was a familiar line that went like this: "If anyone present knows any reason why these two should not be lawfully joined together, let him speak now or forever hold his peace." Although long ago edited out of modern ceremonies, the purpose was to allow someone, anyone, a last chance to stop what might not be right. The idea that someone might actually object is almost foreign to us now, and we fear giving some jealous ex-lover or some dysfunctional family member the opportunity to ruin a perfectly good (and very expensive) wedding. Now it seems as if this hopeless war, this arrogance of power, this agony of the earth, this slow unraveling of the American dream for all but the wealthy, has reached critical mass. It has become, with an uneasy suddenness, too much to bear— and too important to keep silent about.

It is as if someone at the prayer breakfast clinked a knife against the side of his glass, stood up, and said, "If anyone present knows any reason why this marriage of greed and religion should not go forward, this cohabitation of Empire and Gospel, this perversion of the heart and soul of faith itself, then let him speak now or forever hold his peace." And the answer came, not from among those assembled, but from a crowd gathered *outside* in the parking lot. Holding candles and singing the only hymn they could all still remember, they said with one rousing voice, *"We object!"*

We object to war in the name of the Prince of Peace. We object to greed in the name of an itinerant teacher who never owned a house or a second pair of sandals. We object to arrogance in the name of one who said, "Why do you call me good? No one is good but God alone" (Mark 10:18). We object to lying and to stealing and to character assassination in the name of one who said that if you have a complaint against our brother, you should go first to be reconciled with your brother.

We object to petulance and impatience being passed off as salt and light. We object to a follower of Jesus insulting the rest of the world for disagreeing with him and then claiming that God had approved his plan to spread freedom and democracy through murder and mayhem disguised as "shock and awe."

We object to the hypocrisy of judging others for their sexual mistakes and then refusing to admit a single mistake of one's own—even though the mistakes are legion and the consequences deadly. We object to profiteering in the name of patriotism and practicing retaliation in the name of one who counseled us to turn the other cheek. We object to peddling fear and loathing of the enemy when the radical call of the Gospel is to love our enemies and pray for them. We object to public displays of piety from men who have been asked to do their good deeds in private and pray in secret.

We object to those who heap up empty phrases but leave the poor to fend for themselves in their time of need. We object to those who store up treasures on earth and tell those who beg for bread to work longer and pray harder. We object to men who serve two masters and then tell us that they serve only one. We object to those who remove the speck from the neighbor's eye but do not see the log in their own. We object to those who say, without ceasing, "Lord, Lord" but do not do the will of the Father. It is time to resist.

To form religious communities of dignified indignance, we must judge churches by the Sermon on the Mount, not by the size, location, or status of the neighborhood. We must ask whether the church exists to serve only its own members or the world for which Jesus gave his life. We must resist all self-serving communities by looking at the budget to see what the priorities really are. We must consider the mission, not the fringe benefits, and ask whether anyone who is "out" is being invited "in."

Sermon on the Mount churches welcome *everyone*, and that includes gays and lesbians. Sermon on the Mount preachers do not cater to the wealthy or pamper the generous. Women are elevated to positions of equality and leadership in Sermon on the Mount churches because Jesus elevated women in his ministry. Individuals who are disabled are provided access to community life in Sermon on the Mount churches, and the weak are lifted up by the strong.

To quote the urgent words of John 4:23: "But the hour is coming, and is now here, when the true worshipers will worship the Father in spirit and truth, for the Father seeks such as these to worship him."

The time has now come for every single American who is indignant over the direction of this country to expresses that indignance in acts of dignified but tangible resistance. We do not have the luxury of unlimited time. We cannot wait until everyone agrees on everything to know that everything we *can* agree on is reason enough for everyone to act! People are dying. The earth is dying. Human hope is dying.

To stop the war, we must withdraw consent in all its forms, including the refusal to sacrifice our children. At the ballot box, we can remove those from power who have betrayed the best of American values and lined their pockets at our expense. In the marketplace, we can refuse to fund what undermines the livelihood of others and destroys the environment. In the church, we can insist on hearing a sermon on the Sermon on the Mount again—or withdraw the consent of our membership.

There is no resistance without sacrifice. Those in power today are convinced that the rest of us have lost the capacity to sacrifice for the common good. They believe that we serve only ourselves and will never lie down in front of the train of history to throw it off the tracks. They are depending on us to go right on consuming mindlessly, living for the moment, wasting the future, and cheering the troops as they march off to war.

If we do, their hold on power will be permanent. If we go on amusing ourselves to death, flicking the TV remote through hours of mind-numbing unreality, frozen in the blue light of isolation, nothing will change. If we go on shopping our way to an oblivion of the soul, we will all perish together in a soulless oblivion. If we do not help to build and to fund and to energize a true opposition party, we may indeed wake up some day to discover that it is too late.

That is, unless we act *now*. Unless we resist *now*. Unless we find or create communities of dignified indignance *now*. For there has come again what Martin Luther King Jr. called "the fierce urgency of now."[22] If we don't do it now, when might we do it? And if we don't do it at all, what are we saying? What have we decided?

That our kids aren't worth it? That God's Creation isn't worth it? That we aren't worth it?

And what is the dream of the prophets? That we should study war no more, that we should beat our swords into plowshares and our spears into pruning hooks. Who would Jesus bomb indeed? How many wars does it take to know that too many people have died? What if they gave a war and nobody came? Maybe one day we will find out.

Time to march again, my friends.

I love this coluntry.

Let's take it back.

Notes

Introduction

1. For more information on the Project for a New American Century, go to http://www.newamericancentury.org. For a critique of the effect of 9/11, see Duane Shank, "The Project for a New American Empire: Who Are These guys? And Why Do They Think They Can Rule the World?" *Sojourners*, Sept.-Oct. 2003.
2. One of many subsequent claims that the UN faced becoming "irrelevant" was made in the president's speech to the UN General Assembly on Sept. 12, 2002.
3. This quote appeared as part of a "Falwell Confidential" e-mail sent to supporters of Jerry Falwell Ministries, a 501(c)(3) nonprofit charitable organization, on July 1, 2004, urging supporters to reelect Bush and contribute to a political action committee called Campaign for Working Families.
4. Bill Moyers, "9/11 and the Sport of God," CommonDreams.org, Sept. 9, 2005 [http://www.commondreams.org/views05/0909-36.html], based on a speech he delivered at the Union Seminary in New York, Sept. 7, 2005.
5. The so-called war against the judiciary is a well-documented phenomenon, using televised Justice Sundays in megachurches, organized by the Family Research Council.
6. Michael Schwartz, quoted in Max Blumenthal, "In Contempt of Courts," *The Nation*, Apr. 11, 2005 [http://www.thenation.com/doc/20050425/blumenthal].

Part One

1. "Open and Affirming" is the UCC designation for a church that has publicly declared its openness to Christians of all sexual orientations. More information is available at http://ucc.org.
2. For more information about the rise of the Religious Right in the Republican Party, go to http://theocracywatch.org.
3. Creighton Lovelace, pastor of Danieltown Baptist Church in Rutherford County, North Carolina, posted the message "The Koran needs to be flushed" on a portable display in front of his church.
4. According to the best-selling books by Tim LaHaye and Jerry Jenkins, those who are "left behind" after Jesus instantly raptures the faithful will suffer unspeakable horrors. In one novel, *Glorious Appearing*, "Men and women soldiers and horses seemed to explode where they stood. It was as if the very words of the Lord had superheated their blood, causing it to burst through their veins and skin." The authors go on to describe their flesh dissolving, their eyes melting, and their tongues disintegrating.

Part Two

Chapter One

1. Martin Luther King Jr., "I Have a Dream," speech delivered on Aug. 28, 1963, at the Lincoln Memorial in Washington, D.C.
2. Ron Suskind, *The Price of Loyalty: George W. Bush, the White House, and the Education of Paul O'Neill* (New York: Simon & Schuster, 2004), p. 86.
3. Project for a New American Century, "Statement of Principles," June 3, 1997 [http://newamericancentury.org/statementofprin ciples.htm].
4. Interview with Wolf Blitzer, *CNN Late Edition*, Cable News Network, Sept. 8, 2002.

5. Rush Limbaugh, *The Rush Limbaugh Show*, nationally syndicated radio broadcast, June 8, 2005.

6. See James Carroll, "The Bush Crusade," *The Nation*, Sept. 20, 2004 [http://www.thenation.com/doc/20040920/carroll].

7. See Warren P. Strobel, "Iraq Seen Emerging as Prime Training Ground for Terrorists," July 4, 2005 [http://www.krwashington.com].

8. George H. W. Bush, after the shooting down of an Iranian civilian airliner by the U.S. warship *Vincennes*, killing all 290 passengers, quoted in *Newsweek*, Aug. 15, 1989 [http://alternet.org/story/17846].

9. George W. Bush, speech before a joint session of Congress, Sept. 19, 2001 [http://www.washingtonpost.com].

10. Marcus Borg, *Meeting Jesus Again for the First Time* (San Francisco: HarperSanFrancisco, 1994).

11. James Woolsey and Noam Chomsky, "Power Politics," MacNeil/Lehrer Online Forum, Mar. 12, 1998. [pbs.org/newshour/forum/march98/intervention_3–12.html].

12. George H. W. Bush, *A World Transformed* (New York: Knopf, 1998), p. 464.

13. Jean Lacouture, *Le Souverain* (Paris: Éditions de Seuil, 1989), pp. 364–365.

14. During the period between 1967 and 2000, Iraq was the subject of 69 Security Council resolutions. Israel was the subject of 138 resolutions, mostly for violations of basic principles of international law embodied by the UN Charter. For a detailed list, see Michael S. Ladah and Suleiman I. Ajlouni, "Mr. Bush, What About Israel's Defiance of UN Resolutions?" Sept. 29, 2002 [http://mediamonitors.net/michaelsladah&suleimaniajlouni1.html].

Chapter Two

1. Houston Smith, "Reasons for Joy," *Christian Century*, Oct. 4, 2005, pp. 10–11.

2. Fred B. Craddock, emeritus professor of homiletics at the Candler School of Theology in Atlanta, has made this observation in numerous sermons; it is used here with his kind permission.

3. Judge Moore was ultimately removed from office by a unanimous vote of Alabama's judicial ethics panel for defying a federal judge's order to move the Ten Commandments monument from the state supreme court building. Moore said he was not surprised he was being removed from office because he "acknowledged God."

4. For more on the distinctive behaviors of early Christians, see the provocative book by Stephen J. Patterson, *Beyond the Passion: Rethinking the Death and Life of Jesus* (Minneapolis, Minn.: Augsburg Fortress, 2004).

5. J. Paul Getty, quoted in Robert Lenzner, *The Great Getty* (New York: Crown, 1985).

6. Maureen Dowd, *Bushworld: Enter at Your Own Risk* (New York: Putnam, 2004), p. 14.

7. "Christian Leader Condemns Islam: Preacher Franklin Graham Calls Islam 'Wicked, Violent,'" *NBC Nightly News*, Nov. 16, 2001 [http://www.msnbc.com/news/659057.asp].

8. Alan Cowell, "Subway and Bus Blasts in London Kill at Least 37," *New York Times*, July 8, 2005, p. 1.

9. Bob Herbert, "What Bush Doesn't Know," *New York Times*, July 25, 2005, p. 19.

Chapter Three

1. David Kennedy, "The Best Army We Can Buy," *New York Times*, July 25, 2005, p. 19.

2. For a revealing look at the attitude of Young Republicans toward the war, see Adam Smeltz, "Young Republicans Support Iraq War but Not Willing to Join the Fight," Knight Ridder Newspapers, Sept. 1, 2004 [http://www.realcities.com/mld/krwashington/9556221.htm].

3. The report of a congressional probe investigating political advertising began, "It was the most racially charged, divisive TV

ad in the history of presidential campaigns." Eric Engberg, CBS News, Oct. 14, 1992.

4. I was in attendance when this sermon was delivered to a group of Michigan clergy during a preaching worship at Olivet College in 1983.

5. Quoted in "Bush Tells Victims: 'A Lot of Help Coming,'" CNN .com, Sept. 1, 2005 [http://www.cnn.com/2005/POLITICS/08/31/bush.katrina].

6. For a detailed summary on the effect of the Bush tax cuts, see Isaac Shapiro and Joel Friedman, "A Comprehensive Assessment of the Bush Administration's Record on Cutting Taxes," Center for Budget and Policy Priorities, Apr. 23, 2004 [http://www.cbpp.org/4-14-04tax-sum.html].

7. See Jason Byasee, "Be Happy: The Health and Wealth Gospel," Christian Century, July 12, 2005, p. 20.

8. Ibid., p. 21.

9. Ibid., p. 20.

10. Neil Young, "Ohio," copyright © 1970 Neil Young. Reprinted with permission.

11. Marjorie Cohn, "The Quaint Mr. Gonzales," Truthout, Nov. 13, 2004 [http://www.truthout.org/docs_04/111304A.shtml].

12. See Marian Wilkinson, "Prisoner Abuse Rocks America's Faith in Itself," Sydney Morning Herald, May 14, 2004.

13. Bob Herbert, "Who We Are," New York Times, Aug. 1, 2005, p. 15.

14. Ibid.

Chapter Four

1. See Borg, Meeting Jesus Again, pp. 46–47.

2. Bill McKibben, "The Christian Paradox: How a Faithful Nation Gets Jesus Wrong," Harper's, Aug. 2005, p. 31. Used by permission.

3. For more on the idea of a "pre-Easter" and "post-Easter" Jesus, see Borg, Meeting Jesus Again.

4. Ibid., pp. 48–49.
5. This oft-repeated comment is actually a combination of statements made by Vice President Dick Cheney, who said on *Meet
   the Press*, Mar. 16, 2003, that U.S. forces would be greeted as
   "liberators," and the words of Brandeis professor and Iraqi ex-
   patriate Kanan Makiya, speaking at the National Press Club
   the next day, featuring Richard Perle. He said, "As I told the
   president on January tenth, I think they will be greeted with
   sweets and flowers in the first few months and simply have very,
   very little doubts that this is the case."
6. Daniel Yergin, *The Prize: The Epic Quest for Oil, Money, and
   Power* (New York: Free Press, 1993).

Chapter Five

1. George Lakoff, *Moral Politics: What Conservatives Know That Liberals Don't* (Chicago: University of Chicago Press, 1993), ch. 5.
2. Ibid., ch. 6.
3. James Dobson, *Dare to Discipline* (Carol Stream, Ill.: Tyndale
   House, 1970), p. 16.
4. Lakoff, *Moral Politics*, p. 67.
5. Ernest Campbell, quoted in the sermon "We Had to Celebrate,"
   delivered Mar. 25, 2001, at University Baptist Church, Austin,
   Texas [http://ubcaustin.org/sermons/20010325.htm].
6. The 2004 deficit of half a trillion dollars was the largest ever,
   but several others have been worse relative to the nation's gross
   domestic product. As a percentage of GDP, the current deficit
   was in fact equaled or exceeded in four years during the Reagan
   administration and two years in the term of Bush's father—all
   Republicans. See FactCheck.org, "Biggest Deficit in History?
   Yes and No," Feb. 27, 2004 [http://www.factcheck.org/article
   .aspx?docID=148].
7. McKibben, "The Christian Paradox," p. 32.
8. Borg, *Meeting Jesus Again*, p. 47.

9. Samuel Johnson, "Taxation No Tyranny" (1775), in *The Works of Samuel Johnson* (Troy, N.Y.: Pafraets, 1913), vol. 14 [http://samueljohnson.com/america.html].

10. For a detailed review of U.S. relations with Iraq in the 1980s, see Phyllis Bennis, *Understanding the U.S.-Iraq Crisis: A Primer* (Washington, D.C.: Institute for Policy Studies, 2003).

11. See Andrew Kohut, "Anti-Americanism: Causes and Characteristics," Pew Research Center, Dec. 10, 2003 [http://people-press.org/commentary/display.php3?AnalysisID=77].

12. See Abraham J. Heschel, *Between God and Man: An Interpretation of Judaism* (New York: Free Press, 1965).

Chapter Six

1. See Debra Rosenberg and Karen Breslau, "Culture Wars: Winning the 'Values Vote,'" *Newsweek*, Nov. 3, 2003 [http://msnbc.com/id/6401635/site/newsweek].

2. King, "I Have a Dream."

3. John Shelby Spong, *The Sins of Scripture: Exposing the Bible's Texts of Hate to Reveal a God of Love* (San Francisco: HarperSanFrancisco, 2005), p. 113.

4. Ibid., p. 115.

5. Augustine of Hippo, *The Confessions of Saint Augustine*, trans. Edward B. Pusey (Grand Rapids, Mich.: Christian Classic Ethereal Library, 1999), 5.14.24.

6. W. H. Auden, "Christmas Oratio," in *For the Time Being: A Christmas Oratorio* (New York: Faber & Faber, 1945).

7. The first cases of AIDS were identified in 1981, and Reagan was slow to respond, especially during the critical years of 1984 and 1985. The 1985 death of Rock Hudson changed Reagan's attitude about the disease, but his first public comments did not come until February 1986. By 1987, nearly twenty-four thousand Americans had died of AIDS.

8. After Swaggart was photographed entering a seedy hotel outside New Orleans in the company of a known prostitute, Debra Murphree said in an interview that he spoke of including her nine-year-old daughter in sexual activity.

9. Spong, *Sins of Scripture*, p. 140.

10. Alison Mitchell, "Lott Says Homosexuality Is a Sin and Compares It to Alcoholism," *New York Times*, June 16, 1998, p. 24.

11. For a critique of Cameron's research, see Bob Moser, "Holy War," Southern Poverty Law Center, 2005 [http://www.splcenter.org/intel/intelreport/article.jsp?pid=863].

12. See People for the American Way, "Anti-Gay Politics and the Religious Right: Gays as Enemies of Faith," n.d. [http://www.pfaw.org/pfaw/general/default.aspx?oid=2046].

13. People for the American Way, "Anti-Gay Politics and the Religious Right: The Child Molester Lie," n.d. [www.pfaw.org/pfafw/general/default.aspx?oid=2045].

14. God Is Still Speaking, "Only Recently Did United Church of Christ Learn of Networks' Ultimate Refusal of Ads," Dec. 2, 2004 [http://www.stillspeaking.com/news/release3.html].

15. To view the ads deemed "too controversial" for American television and to review the history of the controversy, go to http://www.stillspeaking.com/resources/indexvis.html.

16. Pat Robertson, *The 700 Club*, Christian Broadcasting Network, Jan. 18, 1995.

17. For an introduction to the thought of Emmanuel Levinas, see Adriaan Peperzak, *To the Other* (Indianapolis, Ind.: Purdue University Press, 1993).

18. Joseph Carroll, "Gallup Poll: Who Supports the Death Penalty?" Death Penalty Information Center, Nov. 16, 2004 [http://www.deathpenalty.org/article.php?scid=23&did=1266].

19. See Paul M. Bischke's "An Eye for an Eye: Get-Tough Laws Under Biblical Scrutiny," *Razor Wire*, Oct.-Nov. 1997 [http://www.november.org/razorwire/rzold/04/0407.html].

20. Ibid.
21. See Walter Wink, "Myth of Redemptive Violence," *Bible in Transmission*, Spring 1999 [http://www.biblesociety.org.uk/exploratory/articles/wink99.doc].

Chapter Seven

1. For a complete review of environmental warning signs, see Tim Appenzeller and Dennis R. Dimick, "Signs from Earth," *National Geographic*, Sept. 2004, pp. 2–75.
2. Spong, *Sins of Scripture*, pp. 55–56.
3. Robert F. Kennedy Jr., "Crimes Against Nature," *Rolling Stone*, Dec. 11, 2003 [http://commondreams.org/views03/1120-01.html].
4. Kelly Galagher, "The Truth About Mercury," *Yogi Times*, Apr. 2005 [http://yogitimes.com/04_2005/interview.html].
5. Letter from the Reverend Bob Jones III, congratulating President Bush on his reelection, Nov. 3, 2004.
6. OnLine NewsHour, "Warming Up," Public Broadcasting Service, June 7, 2001.
7. Union of Concerned Scientists, "Restoring Scientific Integrity in Policy Making," Feb. 19, 2004 [http://www.americanprogress.org/site/pp.asp?c=biJRJ8OVF&b=33731].
8. Wes Allison, "Mountains of Debate," *Saint Petersburg* (Fla.) *Times*, Sept. 26, 2004, p. 1A.
9. Matthew Fox, *The Coming of the Cosmic Christ* (New York: HarperCollins, 1988).
10. Wayne Boulton, "The Thoroughly Modern Mysticism of Matthew Fox," *Christian Century*, Apr. 28, 1990, p. 428.
11. Archibald MacLeish, "Bubble of Blue Air," *Riders on the Earth: Essays and Recollections*, epigraph (Boston: Houghton Mifflin, 1978), p. xiv.

Chapter Eight

1. Bush made this comment during a prime-time news conference, Apr. 13, 2004.
2. See Noam Chomsky, "Rogue States," *Z Magazine*, Apr. 1998 [http://www.zmag.org/chomsky/articles/z9804-rogue.html].
3. George Orwell, *1984* (Orlando, Fla.: Harcourt Brace, 1949), pp. 158–159.
4. "The Holy Warrior," CBS News, Sept. 15, 2004 [http://www.cbsnews.com/stories/2004/09/15/60II/main643650.shtml].
5. Ibid.
6. Paul Wood, "Hunting 'Satan' in Falluja Hell," BBC News World Edition, Nov. 23, 2004 [http://news.bbc.co.uk/2/hi/middle_east/4037009.stm].
7. Tom Allard, "Film Rolls as Troops Burn Dead," *Sydney Morning Herald*, Oct. 19, 2005 [http://commondreams.org/headlines05/1019-05.html].
8. Quoted in Moyers, "9/11 and the Sport of God."
9. John C. Danforth, "In the Name of Politics," *New York Times*, Mar. 30, 2005.
10. Jim Wallis, "God's Own Party?" *Sojourners*, May 12, 2005 [http://tompaine.com/articles/20050512/gods_own_party.php].
11. George W. Bush, Keynote Address, Republican National Convention, Madison Square Garden, New York, Sept. 2, 2005.

Chapter Nine

1. Quoted in David R. Francis, "Why the Healthcare Crisis Won't Go Away," *Christian Science Monitor*, July 18, 2005 [http://csmonitor.com/2005/0718/p.17so1-wmgn.html].
2. For an analysis of the Harry and Louise commercials, see *Media Watch*, Aug. 1994 [http://secure.mediaresearch.org/news/mediawatch/1994/mw19940801ana.html].
3. See Walter Brueggemann, Sharon Parks, and Thomas H. Grooms, *To Act Justly, Love Tenderly, and Walk Humbly* (Mahwah, N.J.: Paulist Press, 1986), p. 5.

4. Malcolm Gladwell, "The Moral Hazard Myth: The Bad Idea Behind Our Failed Health-Care System," *New Yorker*, Aug. 29, 2005 [http://newyorker.com/fact/content/articles/050829fa_fact].
5. Ibid.
6. Ibid.
7. Ibid.
8. Mrs. Bush was accompanying her husband, former president George H. W. Bush, on a tour of hurricane relief centers in Houston when she made this widely reported comment, Sept. 5, 2005.
9. Cornel West, "Exiles from a City and from a Nation," *Observer*, Sept. 11, 2005 [http://observer.guardian.co.uk/comments/story/0,6903,1567247,00.html].
10. James J. Mongon, "Healthcare as a Moral Imperative," *Boston Globe*, Nov. 27, 2004.

Chapter Ten

1. Lawrence Britt, "Fascism Anyone?" *Free Inquiry*, Spring 2003, p. 20.
2. Moyers, "9/11 and the Sport of God."
3. For more on the concept of "overhearing" Scripture, see Fred B. Craddock, *Overhearing the Gospel* (Nashville, Tenn.: Abingdon Press, 1978).
4. Moyers, "9/11 and the Sport of God."
5. Matthew Rycroft, "The Downing Street Memo," July 23, 2002, which indicated that war with Iraq was seen as inevitable but was not supported by an imminent threat from weapons of mass destruction or an Iraq-terrorism connection. Hence "the intelligence and facts were being fixed around the policy."
6. Moyers, "9/11 and the Sport of God."
7. For a more complete list of quotes from the Right blasting liberal judges, see Thomas B. Edsall, "Political Leaders Seek to End Gay, Abortion Rights," *Washington Post*, Aug. 15, 2005.

8. Comments made at Justice Sunday II, Two Rivers Baptist Church, Nashville, Tenn., Aug. 14, 2005. For a revealing look at the new alliance between conservative Catholics and the Christian Right, see Carol Eisenberg, "Event Spotlights Growing Catholic, Evangelical Alliance," *Manhattan News*, Aug. 14, 2005.

9. Gene C. Gerard, "Bush Judicial Nominations Are Hardly Mainstream," *Modern Tribune*, Mar. 7, 2005 [http://selvesandothers .org/articles8717.html]. Used by permission.

10. Ibid.

11. CNN, "Bush Nominates Bolton as U.N. Ambassador," Mar. 8, 2005 [http://www.cnn.com/2005/US/03/07/bolton].

12. Ontario Consultants on Religious Tolerance, "Canada: Jimmy Swaggart Criticized for Homophobic Remarks," June 14, 2005 [http://www.religioustolerance.org/hom_news_05b.htm]. Swaggart made his comments on Sept. 12, 2004.

13. All Niebuhr quotes in this chapter are from Arthur Schlesinger Jr., "Forgetting Reinhold Niebuhr," *New York Times*, Sept. 18, 2005.

14. Graham Nash, "Chicago," copyright © 1970 Graham Nash. Reprinted with permission.

Part Three

1. Moyers, "9/11 and the Sport of God."

2. For a concise list of just-war principles and resources for additional study, see "Principles of the Just War" [http://www.mtholy oke.edu/acad/intrel/pol116/justwar.htm].

3. Anthony Lake, assistant to the president for national security affairs, remarks at George Washington University, "Defining Mission, Setting Deadlines: Meeting New Security Challenges in the Post–Cold War World," Mar. 6, 1996.

4. For more information about this growing movement, see Sally Heron, "Building a Vibrant Counter-Recruitment Movement,"

Non-Violent Activist, May-June 2005 [http://warresisters.org/nva 0505-1.htm].

5. King, "I Have a Dream."
6. Martin Luther King Jr., "Beyond Vietnam: A Time to Break Silence," speech delivered at the Riverside Church, Apr. 4, 1967.
7. Thomas Frank, *What's the Matter with Kansas? How Conservatives Won the Heart of America* (New York: Metropolitan Books, 2004).
8. Ibid., p. 6.
9. John Steinbeck, *The Grapes of Wrath* (New York: Viking, 1939), p. 28
10. Quoted in Linda Valdez, "Jesus Would Vote Democratic," *Seattle Post-Intelligencer*, Aug. 18, 2005 [http://seattlepi.nwsource.com/opinion/236940_liberalsop.html].
11. Frank, *What's the Matter with Kansas?* p. 248.
12. Jeffrey Kluger, "Global Warming: The Culprit?" *Time*, Oct. 3, 2005 [http://time.com/archive/preview/0,1109337,00.html].
13. For a thorough cost-benefit analysis of reducing global warming, see Patricia Glick, "Global Warming: The High Cost of Inaction," Sierra Club, c. 1995 [http://www.sierraclub.org/globalwarming/get_involved/inaction.asp].
14. Ronald Reagan, remarks to the Republican National Convention, New Orleans, Aug. 15, 1988 [http://www.reagansheritage.org/reagan/html/reagan_rnc_88.shtml].
15. See Paul Tillich, *The Dynamics of Faith* (New York: HarperCollins, 1957).
16. Henri Nouwen, lecture given at the United Church of Christ Consultation on Parish Ministry, Jan. 1992. For more on Nouwen's life and thought, see *Henri Nouwen: Writings* (Oceanside, Calif.: Orbis Books, 1998).
17. Henry David Thoreau, *Walden, or Life in the Woods* (New York: New American Library, 1999), p. 72. Originally published in 1845.

18. Ibid., pp. 17, 73, 108.
19. Henry David Thoreau, "Life Without Principle," originally published in 1863.
20. Henry David Thoreau, "Civil Disobedience," originally published in 1849.
21. Charles Marsh, "Wayward Christian Soldiers," *New York Times*, Jan. 20, 2006, p. 17.
22. King, "I Have a Dream."

The Author

Robin Meyers, Ph.D., is senior minister of Mayflower Congregational Church (United Church of Christ) in Oklahoma City, Oklahoma. A syndicated columnist and an award-winning commentator for National Public Radio, he has appeared on *Dateline NBC* with Bill Moyers, *ABC World News Tonight*, and numerous PBS programs and was featured in the HBO documentary "The Execution of Wanda Jean," a disturbing look at the injustice and immorality of the death penalty. Meyers writes for *The Christian Century* and is a professor of rhetoric at Oklahoma City University. He and his wife, Shawn, live in Oklahoma City and have three children.